# A VOICE IN HER TRIBE
## A Navajo Woman's Own Story

by
Irene Stewart

Foreword
by
Mary Shepardson

Edited
by
Doris Ostrander Dawdy

BALLENA PRESS

ISBN  0-87919-088-4

Printed in the United States of America.
5th Printing

# Table of Contents

# Illustrations

Cover:  Irene Stewart, 1965.
        Photograph:  John D. Wallace


Following text

Figures

1.  Irene Stewart, 1965.
    Photograph:  John D. Wallace

2.  Greyeyes Stewart, 1965.
    Photograph:  John D. Wallace

3.  Greyeyes Stewart on his beloved (if troublesome) horse, 1965.
    Photograph:  John D. Wallace

4.  Girls' Puberty Ceremony, 1956.  The mother moulds the girl.
    Photograph:  Franciscan Fathers

5.  Girls' Puberty Ceremony, 1956.  The girl blesses a child.
    Photograph:  Franciscan Fathers

6.  Girls' Puberty Ceremony, 1956.  The ritual cake is prepared.
    Photograph:  Franciscan Fathers

7.  Scott Preston, Vice-chairman of the Navajo Tribal Council,
    and Annie Wauneka, Delegate.  Nazlini Chapter House
    Dedication, June 30, 1962.
    Photograph:  John D. Wallace

8.  Canyon de Chelly.  Irene was born in this canyon.
    Photograph:  John D. Wallace

9.  Spider Rock, Canyon de Chelly.  Spider Woman lives on
    top of the tallest pinnacle.
    Photograph:  John D. Wallace

# Foreword

It was a windy day with snow flurries in the air when, in March of 1955, I knocked on the door of a small house near Garcia's Trading Post in Chinle, Arizona. I was in search of the local candidate for the Navajo Tribal Council. Mrs. Greyeyes (Irene) Stewart came to the door, smiled, and when I introduced myself as a graduate student in anthropology from Stanford University, she agreed to answer my questions about her campaign and the forthcoming tribal elections. Her replies were slow, pleasant, reasonable, and her manner was restrained as befitted a woman of her grave and dignified tribe. She had embarked upon a serious undertaking to which she had given much thought. To the stranger from "outside" she patiently explained the problems facing the *Dine'é*, or People, and what she believed she could accomplish for her community and her tribe if she were elected to a seat on the Council.

"You see, we have only one woman councilman, Mrs. Annie Wauneka. The women in Chinle seem to be interested in my campaign. They tell me they want more women on the Council. I was particularly happy because my son wrote me from Intermountain School that he hoped I would be elected because Navajos needed more women delegates."

Irene Stewart told me she was a Christian, and when I asked if this would hurt her chances for election she said, "I don't think so. Although I don't go to Navajo ceremonies, I never try to destroy other people's religion. I'm always working around Chinle. The people here get me to do things."

Chinle, in 1955, was a small, government-centered community in the middle of the enormous Navajo Reservation. The 75 miles of unpaved road that lay between Chinle and Window Rock offered the traveller many road hazards: wash-boards, deep sand, mud holes; and after heavy snows or prolonged rain the road was impassable. There was a government building, a post office, an old Indian boarding school reminiscent of a medieval fortress, a tiny one-room state schoolhouse, two trading posts, a Catholic Mission and a Presbyterian Mission, a small clinic, a lodge for tourists (capacity 18 guests), and a Park Service headquarters with a superintendent and a maintenance man to administer the national monument of Canyon de Chelly (pronounced de Shay). In the Chinle School District there were 1700 residents; in Chinle's Navajo Tribal Council election district there were some 1100 adults. Most of the Navajos lived on farms in the Chinle Wash, or grazed their sheep some distance from Chinle.

Chinle itself is drab with flat stretches of sand, but Canyon de Chelly is one of the stunning natural sights of this beautiful Indian reservation.  It combines many miles of winding canyon, a thousand feet deep at Spider Rock, with hundreds of *Anasazi* cliff ruins (homes of the Ancient Ones as the Navajos call them) set high like jewels in the caves of the red rock walls, with a bright green border of peach trees, cotton-woods, and corn fields along the base of the cliffs.  Navajos cultivate their fields and herd their flocks here in the summertime, but in winter they must move to other hogans on the canyon rim.  Nostalgics and ro-mantics recall with a pang the picturesque sight of Navajo women in their bright-colored plush blouses and long satin skirts riding horseback in the canyon, and the echoing from cliff to cliff of the Navajo Riding Song.

Canyon de Chelly is an historic spot, the heartland of Navajo resistance to the threat of Spaniard and Anglo.  Only by destroying their fields, cutting down their orchards, and driving off the flocks was Kit Carson with his United States Army troops and his enemy Indian allies successful in forcing the surrender of a proud and warlike people.  In 1863, the Navajos were removed to Fort Sumner beyond the Pecos River, and they were allowed to return to their sacred homeland and their Can-yon only after the signing of the Treaty of 1868.  The principal figures whom we will meet in Irene Stewart's narrative are the descendants of these old Canyon families.

My first interview with Irene Stewart in 1955 marked the be-ginning of an acquaintanceship which--over the years, as I returned again and again to Chinle for further studies--grew into a deep and en-during friendship between two women across the cultural divide.  Together we attended meetings, interviewed old medicine men and retired judges of the Navajo Tribal Courts, visited Chapters in other communities, ob-served the Tribal Council in session at Window Rock, with Irene acting as guide, interpreter, and friend.  She seemed at home in both cultures. At rodeos and Tribal Fairs she usually wore a velvet blouse and long satin skirt, her hair done in the special knot bound with wool which is the characteristic "national" hair style.  At church she wore "Anglo" clothes.  As warehouseman distributing grain she donned Levis and a plaid cowboy shirt.  Sometimes we went on "expeditions" for pure enjoy-ment, such as a trip to the *Lukachukai* Rodeo in a picturesque spot up against the mountains, or for a picnic on the canyon rim, or for a dress-up dinner at Thunderbird Lodge, now modernized into a motel and public dining room.

Because Irene is an active member of the Chinle Presbyterian Church, I spent many hours with her and other church members in the manse where I gratefully and joyfully accepted the hospitality and good company of an intelligent and self-sacrificing couple, the Reverend and Mrs. Joseph Gray.  Irene took a leading part in the Navajo church service, in the hymn singing, in teaching classes, in planning dinners and camp meetings, in interpreting at times for Reverend Gray.

My friendship with Irene grew perhaps because we were of the same age and had both lived through many of the same joys and disappointments, failures and successes--the universals of human life. Or perhaps it grew because we shared an intense interest in the building of self-government in our country's largest Indian society, a tribe which is at the same time a "domestic dependent nation." Perhaps we became fast friends simply because we enjoyed each other.

In 1965, after a trip to the reservation, I conceived the idea of asking Irene Stewart to write her life story. By this time the National Institute of Health and the University of Chicago were sponsoring and financing my work on the political and legal life of Navajos, and I was sure that the experiences of that rare person, a Navajo woman community and tribal political leader, would be as interesting and significant to others as it was to me. The narrative that follows is Irene's response to my request. Her story was written to me in a series of letters. Doris Dawdy has edited these letters, revising the order where my questions induced Irene to weave back and forth in time. Some of the spelling and grammar has been changed in order to give the reader a better sense of the status Irene occupies in her own society and culture. But Mrs. Dawdy has, I feel, been able quite successfully to preserve the flavor of Irene's speech and personality as she describes her experiences and expresses her feelings in her own words.

I should like to thank Robert W. Young for his assistance in transcribing the Navajo words according to the Young-Morgan (tribal government-US government system). The late John D. Wallace, the Franciscan Fathers, James Bosch, and Joseph Gray have provided me with pictures over the years, some of which appear in this book.

Mary Shepardson
Palo Alto, California

# Chapter 1

# In The Beginning

Long ago, *Dine'é* (The People), as we call ourselves to identify us from other tribes and races, were wandering groups of people far to the north. Somehow a group wandered as far as *Dibé N Tsah* (La Plata Mountains of Colorado). Others went beyond there to a place called *Ha'atiin* (Road Up Out), where the great tribe came together and held a council to decide upon a permanent place to settle. In those days my people were led by war chiefs and peace chiefs.

The council lasted a long time, with many talks and arguments, for the chiefs and their people could not reach an agreement. A major quarrel developed over which direction they should settle. This was followed by separation of The People into several groups, each headed by a war chief. One group, which had become very angry, moved to the northeast. They are called *Dinénáhódlóonii* (The Other People). The group which moved to the far north is called *Dine'é Bééxai* (Winter People). Those who moved west are *Dine'é Shash* (Bear People); those who moved south are the Apaches.

Only the Navajos stayed where the quarrel took place, from there spreading over a wide area. Quite a large group wandered into the area of our present reservation. Canyon de Chelly became their stronghold. Among these people were my forefathers. They came here seeking a place to hide from their warring enemies--the Utes, Spaniards, Mexicans, Comanches, Apaches, and some Pueblos. Here they were able to protect themselves from all but the Americans who took them as prisoners of war to *Hwééldi* (Fort Sumner) in 1863. During that siege my grandparents had the experience of climbing up one of the dangerous rock fortresses near *Tsé táá'á* (Rock Bends Into Water).

# Chapter 2

## Birth and Childhood

It was at *Tsé táá'á* in Canyon de Chelly that I was born in 1907. Mine was a typical Navajo birth in a hogan, far away from a hospital. Father described my birth this way: "You were born early in spring, when the wind blew hard. As soon as the midwife uttered, 'It's a girl,' your grandmothers named you *Glį nezbah* (Goes to War With)." Later on I was christened by a white missionary and named Irene Elinor, but I kept my Navajo name until I went to the off-reservation school. My older half-sister, *Asdzą́ą́ Tso* (Big Girl), told me Father wanted so much that I would be a boy.

The birth of a Navajo child is an exciting affair. In a warm hogan a mound of sand is made and covered with a cloth or blanket. The mother is seated upon it. She grasps a rope suspended from the ceiling for support and strength as she labors. A midwife is seated in front of her to help get the child born. Some Navajo women still use this method, but more go to a modern hospital.

As soon as the baby appears the midwife cuts off the umbilical cord. This is followed by a cold water bath for a fresh beginning in life. Afterward the baby is wrapped in a warm blanket and placed near the fire for warmth, and the mother is given warm cornmeal gruel for strength.

Once I saw the birth of twin boys in the Navajo way. The mother, though weak from labor, uttered, "My dear baby" after each boy appeared. My husband Greyeyes told me this was an ancient customary greeting to a new-born baby. I never uttered these words to my sons at their births because I didn't know of the custom then. Also, they were born in a modern hospital.

Long before the birth of a child the expectant mother has a *Hozhǫǫjí* (Blessing Way) ceremony performed over her so that all will be well for the mother and the baby. It is a two-day affair.

At the birth of a child Blessing Way songs are sung by the medicine man. Neighbors, friends, and relatives gather for this important event. After the baby is born the midwife and the medicine man are paid for their services, and a feast and gift-giving follow. This is to endow the child with good qualities of character, especially generosity and

hospitality. After this the father or some relative makes a cradle
board from a perfect tree--one not struck by lightning.

A portion of the tree is cut into two long pieces the length
of the baby and one piece for the footboard. A thin piece of cedar or
oak is narrowed down for the hood and bent to form a curve. Buckskin
or cloth is hung over the curve to form a canopy. Each piece is tied
together with buckskin or string. At the sides of the cradle board are
lacing strings to tie the baby in the cradle, eight or ten to each side.
The mattress is made from shreds of cedar bark, old clothes, a pillow,
or a blanket. Lacing starts from the top. Every bit of material is
touched with corn pollen and sheep tallow with red ochre as the maker
prays. The cradle board is convenient and safe and comfortable. I was
raised in one.

In the year of 1910 my mother died after giving birth to a boy.
The baby lived only two days. Father was away, working on the railroad;
he got home after Mother was buried.

After Mother's death, Grandmother *Asdzą́ą́ Ts'osi* of *Tótsohnii*
Clan (Big Water People) took me. I was only four years old. Being
brought up by my grandmother led to a very close relationship between us.
I can remember how I snuggled close to her at bed time. My sister *Asdzą́ą́
Tsoh* said she hardly let me out of her sight.

My grandmother took me on her back to go places. I recollect
that once we walked out to Chinle* with some other women over eleven or
twelve miles of sand. I must have been nearly six years old. I tried
my best to keep up with them, but they had to take turns hauling me on
their backs. That summer must have been very dry because the wind blew
so much sand. We became very thirsty and someone dug deep into the sand
close to the canyon wall for water. We dipped with our hands and drank.

On the way to Chinle, we met up with an old woman who had no
nose. Her name was *Asdzą́ą́ Chííshch'įįdii*. When she talked it was with
a gutteral sound. I didn't understand her, but Grandmother talked with
her.

I can remember how, when these old women met, they embraced one
another and cried so loud, telling of their not seeing each other for a
long time and that it was a pleasure to meet again. They would inquire
about each other's health, the state of hogan life, the news about other
relatives, friends, neighbors. The old people still do this, but not the
younger generation.

When *Chííshch'įįdii* (Snub-nosed) noticed me she wanted to know
all about me. Grandmother told her whose daughter I was. She extended
her hand for me to come to her, but I was afraid and began to cry and
hide my face against my grandmother. I never saw *Chííshch'įįdii* again,

---

*\*Ch'ínílí* (It flows out): mouth of Canyon de Chelly.

though I often thought of her in later years.

I told my husband Greyeyes about this experience. He said,
"I know she was my relative on my father's side, and is related to *Mą'ii
Deeshghiizhnii* (Coyote-Pass-People, the Jemez Indians). Two of her
daughters are living at the foot of the White House Trail in Canyon de
Chelly, *Asdzą́ą Holǫ* (Sophie Price) and *Dzaani Łitsóí*. They are of Coyote
Clan." *Asdzą́ą Holǫ* went to school with my sister *Asdzą́ą Tsoh* at Fort De-
fiance where they completed fifth grade. *Dzaani Łitsóí* is uneducated.
Both daughters have always had sheep and are fine rug weavers.

At Chinle, I saw for the first time a trading post (*naalyéhé
bá'hooghan*). I didn't want to go inside because I was afraid of strange
people, especially white people, so we sat and rested under a cottonwood
tree near the store. I remember seeing a tall Navajo girl dressed in
school clothes. She had long braided hair hanging down her back. Grandmother said she was a school girl working for the people at the trading
post.

Some years later I learned that this trading post belonged to
Nelson Gorman and his wife Alice. Nelson belongs to *Kinyaa'áanii* Clan
(Towering House People); his wife to *Dibéłizhiní* (Black Sheep) Clan.

13

# Chapter 3

## School and White People

My childhood in the Canyon was fun.  I was fed fresh goat's milk and other Navajo food.  All was play.  My close cousin *Dzaani Łitólí* (Crystal Girl) was two or three years older than I.  We were playmates.  After I was taken away to school she was not forgotten.  I missed her so much.  She still lives right where we used to live.  Her hair is now grayer than mine.

I do not remember much of my early life in the Canyon.  I was far away from school and white people.  With the love of my grandmother I felt secure.  This is how it was when all of a sudden I was snatched away from those who loved and cared for me--away from my beloved home place, Rock Bends Into Water.

Father told me that one fall day around noon, a mounted Navajo policeman came.  I was in the care of my near cousin *At'ééd Tsoh* because my grandmother had gone to the canyon rim to pick yucca fruit and cactus berries to dry for winter food.  She couldn't take me along because she had to go on foot.

The policeman took me on horseback all the way to the school at Fort Defiance.  My father said that Grandmother wouldn't give me up to be put in school so he had told the agency superintendent, Peter Paquette, to send a policeman to pick me up.  Years later I was told that Grandmother took this very hard, and that her dislike for Father increased.  Because of this she moved to Tuba City, taking with her all near relatives, except two girls who got married to young men living near Chinle.  They were residing where we used to live and now their grandchildren own the place.

This sudden change in my life was a shocking experience.  From a primitive, wild, Navajo life into a strange place with strange people, food, clothing.  I was homeless.  No one cared for me as my old home folks had.  I feared everything, especially the people and the strange facilities.

Upon being brought into the girls' home, I was taken to a huge bathtub full of water.  I screamed and fought but the big girl in charge was too strong.  She got me in and scrubbed me.  Then she put me into underwear and a dress with lots of buttons down the back.  I remember how

15

she combed my hair until it hurt.  And the shoes she put on my feet were so strange and heavy.  I was used to moccasins.

At night we were put to bed in beds that seemed so high.  Some of us fell out during our sleep.  There was always someone crying, mostly because of homesickness.  One time I cried all night long because I had an earache; it was so painful.

During my first winter in school I became very ill with double pneumonia which nearly took away my life.  I was put in the hospital where a kind missionary nurse took care of me.  I remember how she forced jello into my mouth, the first jello I had ever seen.

Miss Shirley was my teacher.  She was kind to us, and her teaching was such that we loved to learn.  She taught us with colored balls.  This is how I learned there were all kinds of colors.  She divided her pupils into what she called her Baby Class, Sunbeam Class, and Big Class.

At the end of the school year, Grandmother came after my older sister who had completed five years of schooling.  I thought I would be taken along but Grandmother said that my father would take me because he had legal charge of me.  He had not arrived so I became frightened and hysterical.  I hung onto my sister, begging not to be left behind.  Finally, Grandmother talked with the school superintendent through an interpreter and obtained permission to take me with her.

After having lunch at the trading post, we left for Ganado in a buckboard wagon owned and driven by a woman relative.  I was so tired from crying that I slept most of the way to Saint Michaels, about ten miles from Fort Defiance.  Late in the evening we reached Cross Canyon where the woman told Grandmother she would have to leave us as she was going in another direction.  From there we walked through a forest to the home of some people whom Grandmother knew.  It was dark and I fell into the brush even though I held onto Grandmother.  As we neared the home, dogs attacked us.  This was very frightening and I began to cry.  Finally, a man came out and called the dogs.  I learned later that he was our clan relative.

The people were very happy to see my grandmother.  I don't remember their names, but I have never forgotten the old woman who expressed her concern about me, saying to Grandmother, "Are you taking her all the way to Tuba City?  She is too small for the long trip."  I didn't care how far away Tuba City was just so long as I was with my home folks.

Early in the morning I was awakened for breakfast.  My sister shook me, saying, "Get up!  Your father is here."  I wasted no time getting up and jumping into his arms.  As soon as we had breakfast and the horse was saddled, we went back to Fort Defiance.  I was happy to go with Father because I loved him, but it was my final parting with Grandmother for she passed away before I had a chance to see her again.

On the way back to Fort Defiance, where we were to be with my father's brother, Lewis Watchman, Father said he would like to have me go on to school even though I would be lonesome.  He said, "You have no one but me. Your mother has been dead these three years. Someday you will take advantage of your education."

I remember entering elementary school in a large building where the studies were very hard for me. The teachers were mean and strict. We were always being punished for not knowing our lessons. Once I was slapped in the face for gazing out of the window, and once for chewing gum in class. We were never allowed to talk to one another in school, or to speak our language where we could be overheard.

During the day we were always being put in line to march to school, to meals, to work, to the hospital. Four hours of each day were for school work; four hours for industrial education. Saturday afternoons were for play; Sundays, we went to church. Getting our industrial education was very hard. We were detailed to work in the laundry and do all the washing for the school, the hospital, and the sanitorium. Sewing was hard, too. We learned to sew all clothing, except underwear and stockings, and we learned to mend and darn and patch. We canned food, cooked, washed dishes, waited on tables, scrubbed floors, and washed windows. We cleaned classrooms and dormitories. By the time I graduated from the sixth grade I was a well-trained worker. But I have never forgotten how the steam in the laundry made me sick; how standing and ironing for hours made my legs ache far into the night. By evening I was too tired to play and just fell asleep wherever I sat down. I think this is why the boys and girls ran away from school; why some became ill; why it was so hard to learn. We were too tired to study.

During the third year of elementary school, a missionary named Mr. Black took us into his home for almost three years. His mother had died in an accident near Gallup on her way from the east to live with him. It was due to his grief that Mr. Black decided to care for us and to fill his lonely life. We knew him through Uncle Lewis who did all the interpreting for him and other Protestant missionaries. At his home I had the privilege of learning out of Old Mother Goose books and singing songs while he and Jim Damon played the guitar. We had become very attached to Mr. Black, and it was a sad parting for us when he married Nellie Damon and we returned to the government dormitory.

During the closing years of school days at Fort Defiance I began taking part in school programs--something I was too shy to do before. These programs were given at Thanksgiving, Christmas, Easter, and just before school closed. I remember my fifth grade teacher calling me aside at four o'clock one afternoon. She said, "You have been chosen to sing a song with a boy on Easter Sunday." I was so surprised. Me sing with a boy? Before, I had sung only with a group.

I had a high-pitched voice which sometimes cracked when I recited or read aloud. The girls used to make fun of me. They would say, "Be sure and lower your voice so we won't get frightened." However, the song, which was entitled "Lilies of Easter," went over well. The boy and I sang the duet and the rest of the class sang the chorus. The auditorium was full of students, employees, traders, and missionaries. We were told that we sang beautifully. From then on I was interested in singing, and

began learning alto parts.  Singing in groups or in choirs is something
I continued to do throughout the years.

When I look back at my elementary school days, I remember that
there were happy times when we played on merry-go-rounds and swings;
when we played follow-the-leader, somersault, and jacks; when we skipped
rope and played with rag dolls.  We made snowmen, threw snowballs, and
skated in the winter.  During evenings we told Navajo stories.  By the
time I entered fifth grade I had forgotten about my grandmother and other
relatives.  I was no longer always lonesome and homesick.  And when I
was home on summer vacations, I missed the fun I had at school.

A Navajo boy or girl is told not to play too much for too much
playing will cause one to become a negligent and neglectful person.  So
I learned to herd sheep, prepare wool, and weave; to clean the hogan floor
and wash dishes; to clean myself, wash my hair, and keep it combed and
braided; to make my own dresses (sewing by hand), wash clothes, cook,
milk goats, haul buckets of water (not too heavy); and when there was a
garden I hoed and watered the plants.

Navajos wash their hair often with yucca soap suds to clean and
soften their hair, but I was allergic to this wild plant.  To check the
itching I applied tallow all over my head and face.  I was told that store
soap would cause dandruff and falling hair, and would not remove all the
dirt.  To further improve my hair--for Navajo women and girls admire
thick, long hair--it was brushed until it got glossy.  Then my stepmother
tied it in a knot.

My stepmother taught me a very different way of sewing from what
I learned at school.  There I learned to use patterns and go by measure-
ments, cutting and sewing both by hand and by machine.  Stepmother simply
took the goods, tore it into several lengths for my skirt, and for the
blouse she cut only where she could not tear.  When she sewed them together they fitted correctly; only the hem remained to be done.  All of
this was done by hand as we did not have a sewing machine.  I learned to
sew fine seams, so neat that the stitches could hardly be seen.  I was
proud of the first dress I made.

My father was the one who taught me how to grow up to be a good
girl.  "Pay attention to good teachings and practice them," he said.
"Stealing and lying are bad; you must not keep company with girls who do
these things.  You must not mistreat little girls younger than you.  Above
all, don't ever try to run away from school.  You will get into trouble
by so doing, and you know the punishments for this.  Also, if you run off,
there are wild animals in the forests and canyons like bears and wolves.
They eat people."  This I promised not to do for I feared the punishments
meted out to runaways.  They were spanked, and either locked up in a room
or made to walk back and forth in front of the girls and boys' dormitories.
If a boy, he was dressed in girls' clothing; if a girl, in boys' clothing.

I had known about those girls and boys who had tried running
away.  Few succeeded.  The others were caught and brought back.  One boy
ran off in midwinter and froze his feet.  A girl, caught not far from the
school, received a whipping from the head matron.

18

Chapter 4

## Some Recollections of my Girlhood

My father told me that Mother was one of the best weavers in
Canyon de Chelly.  Her rugs and blankets were always of good sizes and
sold for good prices.  She used patterns of trees and birds which at
the time were new and rare for a Navajo weaver.  The so-called sand painting patterns were not used, since the Navajos held the copying of such to
be sacrilegious.

Mother taught my two half-sisters to weave.  My sister *Asdzáá
Tsoh* told me that Mother buried my dried navel cord at the base of her
weaving loom so that I would be a weaver, too.  (A boy's navel cord is
buried in a sheep or horse corral to make him a good herder, and so that
he will have many sheep and horses.)

I have never taken an interest in weaving.  When I was 10 or 11
years of age, I tried to weave at my father's suggestion.  The loom was
just the size for me to practice on.  My father kept a good watch while
I was weaving.  He kept saying, "Watch the ends on both sides; do not pull
the yarn too much, for too much pulling will ruin the straight edges."
Several times I unraveled the yarn.  I had no idea what design to use,
so my stepmother started me on an easy and simple one, mostly stripes.  I
was doing very well until the day a girl cousin came to visit my paternal
grandmother.  Cousin *Ałkéé'yibah* (Warring Together), who was older than
I, said she knew how to weave and asked if she could help me.  I was
anxious to get the blanket done so I let her weave.  The first few lines
were all right so I left to play with my little sister, *Ałnááyibah*.  When
I returned to see how far *Ałkéé'yibah* had helped, I found to my disap-
pointment that she had ruined the edges.  She had not bothered to un-
ravel the yarn.  To undo her work was too much for me and when I finished
the blanket it was wide at each end and pulled in at the middle.  I gave
it to my baby sister for a cradle blanket.  It was kept for many years.
Folks said that I would have been a good weaver if I had kept on, but that
*Ałkéé'yibah* ruined it all.  I never took another try at the art of weaving.

My attempt to live the traditional Navajo way of life was
chopped up with school life.  The customary puberty ceremony was not made
for me because I was in school at that age.  However, I have seen a girl
go through her puberty ceremony.  It was a four days' affair during
which she could not eat salt or sugar or scratch herself.  She was dressed
in her best clothes and her hair was tied up in the middle with a buckskin

string, the hair falling loosely over the shoulder. She had on as much jewelry as she could wear: beads, bracelets, earrings, and a belt of silver over a sash of woven yarn.

During all of the four days the girl was kept busy cooking, cleaning up, and waiting on people. This was to make her industrious. She did all the grinding of corn for the cornmeal cake, a very large one baked in corn husks in the ground during the final night. When the cake was done the following morning, it was opened. The girl cut first from east to west and then south to north to the center. It is customary to give the heart of the cake--the center part--to either the medicine man or a favorite relative or friend. This girl gave it to a boy friend.

The cornmeal-cake ceremony and the singing of Blessing Way songs during the final night were the main events of this four-day affair. The songs were about good fortune--tangible goods such as horses and sheep--to bless the girl with these for her long life. In the morning, after the cake had been distributed to the singers, a model woman was selected to press the girl's body from head to foot while she lay face down on a pile of blankets and shawls of the people gathered there. This was done so she could acquire a pretty shape of body and be beautiful and modest. When she arose white clay was applied to her face--upward on both cheeks--and to her hair. Everyone then grabbed his blankets and went on his way, thus ending the ceremony.

As a child I was shifted back and forth from my Navajo life to the white man's schools, and I think this accounts for some of my varied characteristics. It was in my early years that I began to give way to feelings of inferiority and insecurity. It seemed as though hardly any-one cared for me after I was taken away from Grandmother. I had an un-usual number of fears on into adolescence. I was afraid of darkness, people, lightning, and thunder, and to this day I am afraid of lightning. Three times I was nearly struck by lightning, once so close that I fainted.

It was shortly after this experience that I became sick, and was in bed for two months of my school vacation. I had pains in the lower part of my body and could not get up and walk. I lost my appetite until I was skin and bones. My father gave up all hope for my recovery and moved me away from our regular hogan to a shelter house to die.

During my illness I had strange experiences. There were al-ways visitors during the night--owls, and coyotes howling nearby. During the day the visitors were mice and blue jays. How I got through the nights I don't recall, though Father was with me to keep up the fire. My stepmother took care of me during the day.

There came a time when my father couldn't stand watching me suffer any longer. With tears in his eyes he said to my stepmother, "I am going once more to gather some tree branches and wild herbs and give her a sweat bath with the *Tó ńlóee ńloéetó tóójí*" (Hail and Water Chant, now a forgotten ceremony). At noon he came back with loads of branches and herbs. He built a fire and heated several stones of good size until they were red hot. He put them into a hole in the ground and covered

them with the fresh boughs and herbs.  I was laid upon them and covered
with several blankets.  Every now and then a herb potion was given me to
drink.  This was done until the heat went down and I was taken back to
the shelter.  I slept the rest of the day.  After awakening I felt a
sudden urge to get up.  I was let up, and with some sticks for support
I began to walk.

Two weeks later I returned to school.  When I checked in at
the dormitory my girl friend met me.  She said, "We heard that you died
from some awful sickness and here you are very much alive, but you look
awfully pale and skinny."  I told her I had some kind of lame sickness.
Years later I heard of infantile paralysis and wondered if this is what
I had.

I never went to the hospital when I was sick, because I was
afraid of the doctors.  Also, I had been told that many people died there,
and that there must be a lot of children-ghosts.

Chapter 5

# Uncle Lewis and Cousin Dadi

Lewis Watchman, my father's brother, stands out in my memory of my young days. Uncle Lewis was a very kind, understanding, and educated man. He was one of the young men who went to the Chicago World's Fair in 1893 with Chee Dodge, several uneducated men, and one girl. They were to observe the civilization and education in the modern world of white people, so that they could take an interest in these accomplishments and tell their people about them.

Uncle Lewis made use of his education in those early days by becoming a skilled interpreter for missionaries and agency superintendents.

Uncle Lewis was married to an uneducated woman of *Ashįįhí* Clan (Salt Clan), and they had five children. I was raised with these children, especially the first four. Dadi, the oldest, was five years older than I, but we were very close to each other.

Uncle's home was one of the best. He had a house (which burnt down), a hogan, a chuck house, barns, farm land, cattle, horses, sheep, goats, poultry, and pigs. He kept hired hands to look after his farm. I enjoyed helping with the poultry and herding the sheep.

Uncle was a good cook. When his wife and the hired hands went to the sheep summer camp at Washington Pass for two months, I usually stayed with him. I loved the pies and hash he made. One time, when summer was ending and his wife and the others had moved back, they butchered a sheep and cooked the ribs and the liver for our meal. As we sat at a round table to eat, Uncle's wife, who knew I disliked liver (now my favorite), said, "*Glį nezbah* doesn't like liver; it is good for her; cut her a piece."

When no one was looking I dropped the liver to the house cat sitting at my feet. Then I asked for some fresh rib which was given me. I noticed the others were eating relishes and mustard. I had never tasted mustard before and wondered what it was like. Everyone seemed to like it for they kept saying, "Pass the mustard." Finally I got up enough nerve to say, "Please pass the mustache." Everyone had a good laugh while my uncle pretended to pull his mustache off to hand me.

Cousin Dadi shared her nice room and double bed with me. When she outgrew her nice clothes she gave them to me and I wore them to

23

tatters.  She also gave me some of her old-fashioned dolls.  She was
getting too old for them.  When I was about 16, Dadi got married.  I
felt badly about it.  I thought she should have gone to school; also
I thought she was too young for the man she was marrying.  How sad I was.
No more chum; no more play.

Dadi had a Navajo marriage with the traditional basket ceremony,
and later a Christian marriage.  The basket ceremony marriage is a very
elaborate affair, especially in the old days, and it can only be performed when the girl is a virgin.  Dadi's mother invited all relatives on
both sides, and also the head men around Fort Defiance who were close
friends of Uncle Lewis.  These head men gave instructions to the bride
and groom as to how to get married and live a happy married life and
raise a family.  They instructed the groom more than Dadi.

There was not much gift-giving by the groom to Dadi's folks,
and not all of the old traditions were observed.  Greyeyes told me that
in olden times the marriages were arranged; there was no open courtship.
The head of the family usually chose the mate for the boy, or for the old
man who wanted a young mate.  The chooser would probably say, "There is a
suitable girl or maiden over there at so-and-so's place who is not of our
clan" (de'eyóní).  Then a man who is selected as the escort is sent over
with the mother or the father of the boy or man who is to get a wife, and
it is their job to bring about the marriage proposal.  The gifts to the
family have been agreed upon, usually a  strand of Navajo beads--in the
olden days, shell beads, cedar-seed beads with animal claws, Mexican silver
beads, or red beads--a silver concho belt or yarn belt, ten to twelve
horses (before permit days), and maybe some sheep and goats.

When the marriage is agreeable and has been accepted by the girl's
family and relatives, the date is set and the gifts are delivered.  In
olden days, buckskin, buffalo robes, quiver bags with bows and arrows, and
other valued things were given to men who went hunting or on the war path.
For the women there were Navajo blankets and woven wool dresses.  The
gifts were distributed among the members of the immediate family first,
then to the relatives.

Usually one fat horse is killed for the feast.  The wedding is
performed in the evening.  The groom, dressed for the occasion, is brought
to the new hogan which has been built for the couple by the escort.  He
takes a seat at the middle back part of the hogan to the left side.  The
bride is escorted in by her father who carries a jug of water; she carries
a basket of cooked cornmeal mush, and takes her seat on the right side of
the groom.  From the jar the groom pours water over the bride's hands as
she washes; then she pours water over the groom's hands as he washes.
The basket of cornmeal mush is set before them to eat.  It is first blessed
by the father of the bride.

At Dadi's marriage, Uncle Lewis took yellow corn pollen and drew
a line across the basket from east to west, south to north, and a circle
around the rim of the basket, sunwise.  Following this the groom took a
piece of mush from the east, south, west, and north sides.  The bride did
likewise and then took from the middle.  There was a bowl of water for

24

them to drink. After they had eaten all they wanted, the relatives and visitors finished what was left.

The wedding feast which followed was given by Dadi's family and relatives. The leftovers were taken by the groom's family. Nothing must be left behind.

After the feast was over the head men lectured the newlyweds on living a happy married life and raising a family. They instructed the groom more than Dadi. Then the wedding basket was given to the groom's mother. Dadi's mother was not present because of the mother-in-law taboo.

Dadi's mother kept out of her son-in-law's sight and he kept out of hers. If at any time we thought one of them didn't know the other was near, we yelled, "There's an owl over there." According to the taboo, if they saw one another they would go blind. My father told me that it was very disrespectful for a woman to see her son-in-law. A good mother-in-law will observe this as long as she lives.

Greyeyes said, "The mother-in-law taboo is of mythical origin. First Woman and First Man's Daughter got married. First Woman kept herself hidden from the groom; only First Man saw them get married. After the marriage the groom went away leaving his trail. First Man said to First Woman, 'Our son-in-law has gone; just his tracks are about the place. Come and see.' First Woman objected to even looking at her son-in-law's tracks and said, 'I am ashamed to even take a look at my son-in-law's foot tracks. Why should I look for him or look at him? He belongs to my daughter.' This made it morally binding upon all mothers-in-law."

# Chapter 6

## Four Years at Haskell Institute

On June 2, 1922, I received my first hard-earned diploma. It was the happiest event. I was graduating from the sixth grade at Fort Defiance after long, hard years, although the last two had been happy ones as well. My father had said, "Learn all you can at school. I will not live forever to look after you." Our superintendent, Peter Paquette, told us, "This is only your Commencement Day. Finishing the sixth grade is just the beginning of other school years ahead." Mr. Paquette, who had a genuine interest in us children, was for many years an agent to the Navajo tribe as well as our superintendent. He persuaded all the graduates to continue by enrolling for off-reservation schools.

To Albuquerque, Santa Fe, Phoenix, and Haskell Institute in Lawrence, Kansas, we went. The majority of my classmates didn't want to go as far away as Haskell where, if parents were too poor to pay transportation home for vacations, the students must spend their summers.

When I finally got a chance to stand before the registrar to tell him my preference for Phoenix Indian School, he said that it was full and that only Haskell was open. After we had registered for that school, he said, "You girls and boys are brave to accept this school, but you won't regret going there. It is one of the best Indian schools, with more training and high-school subjects." He told us there were some Navajos there. One boy and three girls whom we knew had relatives there, but they had gone voluntarily. For us there was no choice since the other schools were full.

I told my father that I was determined to continue my education, and that this time no policeman was going to pick me up. I had that youthful fancy to become educated in some off-reservation school among other tribes.

I think my father was proud of my sixth-grade education because he told relatives and visitors that I had finished school at Fort Defiance. One old man who came to visit him thought this might be a fine chance to obtain a young girl for a wife. After he left, Father told my stepmother to tell me about this old man's old-time marriage deal. For the man had already decided on the following gifts for my father: nine goats, a silver belt, and one pair of beads. My father said that no matter how poor he was he was not going to give me to the old red man and so he told him that

I was going to off-reservation school and if I were given to him the agent would surely have the two of us arrested and jailed. The old man had hurried out of the hogan after hearing this, my father said.

We all laughed about what happened, but I was very much embarrassed at the absurdity of being exchanged for those goats. Later on, my stepmother started to worry because the old man was known to be a witch; she was afraid he might cast evil spells on me. I was so afraid that he might come back any day that I asked to go to Uncle Lewis's place and stay with Cousin Dadi. Father assured me that he would not dare come back.

That summer was spent preparing to leave for Haskell. I made two dresses, and Father bought me my first suitcase and a pair of white high-topped shoes. The trading post at the Fort wasn't selling new style shoes yet in 1922, nor was it selling dresses.

There were twelve of us girls and boys who had enrolled in that far-away eastern school. "I am going toward the sunrise," I told my father. He was perplexed over my going so far away from him, parting for four long years, maybe never to see each other again. He reminded me of my recent illness--that of paralysis--saying, "Tell the doctor about it." And he wanted to know why I had enrolled in a school so far away when there were nearer ones.

The day came when we were to go away from our people. With our luggage we piled into an old army truck which was parked in front of the girls' building at Fort Defiance Boarding School. Our folks and school friends stood around to see us off. Just before I climbed in, Father hugged me and blessed me with his corn pollen. I cried as I took my seat.

We traveled on a dirt road, arriving at Gallup about four in the afternoon. We were transferred immediately to two cars at the end of a long locomotive. It took three and one-half days to get to Haskell because the train traveled so slowly. All of us were tired of the journey. We ate our meals on the train. The cook at Fort Defiance had packed three large boxes of sandwiches and some apples for us.

We were not allowed off the train to relax for a few minutes during train stops. I think this was because one of the students was missing when we boarded the train at Gallup. Evidently he sneaked away while the man in charge was buying our tickets.

At noon on the fourth day we arrived at a dingy, isolated platform in a little town near Haskell Institute. There another big army truck awaited us. We were a very tired lot as we piled into the truck for our destination. When I saw the old grey stone buildings of Haskell, I felt disheartened. They were far from my happy imaginings about my new school.

Upon our arrival we were told to hurry up and get ready for the noon meal. We noticed the other students were already in line. I don't remember what was served us; I was car-sick and lonesome, and barely touched my food.

The girls' dormitory impressed me no more than the campus. Our assigned rooms were on the third floor. Another girl and I were led to a large room where eight or nine other girls of different tribes roomed. Not knowing what to do, I sat there without even unpacking my suitcase. I wanted to get away from there and return home. Then the other girl and I broke down and cried. A girl came over and tried to console us, but just then the floor matron appeared. When she saw us crying instead of unpacking, she took us to her room and talked to us. She said there were some Navajos there, two from Fort Defiance and six from Tuba City. It didn't help much; the lonesomeness stayed with me for almost two years.

During the second year, Mr. Paquette came to check on us. We were called into the head matron's office where he was waiting. One girl began to cry, telling Mr. Paquette how much she missed her folks, especially her mother and father. She asked to go back with him, but he said he was on his way east to Washington, D.C. Mr. Paquette said we all looked fine and up in style; some girls had their hair bobbed and used make-up.

At Fort Defiance we dressed in uniforms; at Haskell we wore the clothes we brought from home. There was plenty of clothing issued by the government for those who couldn't afford to buy their own. Sundays everyone dressed in uniforms. We had a military dress parade in the afternoon which was attended by the people from nearby towns.

During my lonesome days I wrote to my uncles about how lonesome I was, and asked them to let me come home. They said, "You will get over it soon; stay there and do your best to finish the four years." Uncle Lewis even went so far as to say, "Learn to bake good cakes; when you come home we can have cakes for our meals."

During that first fall at Haskell in 1922, bobbed hair had come into style. Nearly all the girls had their hair curled and nearly all used make-up. At roll-call the girls were told by the matron not to overdo painting their faces, and to keep skirts below the knees. The rich Oklahoma girls were very much in style, especially the Osage, for they had money from oil. I remember one Osage girl with clean, short hair, cut like a man's. The other girls nicknamed her "Ponjola," the term used for such a haircut. This girl wore a brand-new style of suit that made her look like a man. When I first saw her among the girls in line I thought, "What is that man doing among us?" When I said this to the girl next in line to me, she laughed and answered, "That 'he' is a girl; that is Dottie, the richest girl from Oklahoma."

We Navajo girls did not go out for style for some time because we did not have money. After two years at Haskell I had my hair bobbed. I thought it would take less time to care for, thereby enabling me to be on time for kitchen work in the mornings. Because of being late I had received demerit marks which had to be worked out on Saturday afternoons, a fate in store for all students with demerits.

My Pima Indian girl friend had encouraged me to let her cut my hair, saying how nice and young I would look if I got rid of my long hair. I imagined myself looking like some of the pretty girls who were in style. So one Saturday afternoon I sat on the stool and told her to cut away while I had my eyes closed. As I listened to the whacking noise of cutting, I thought of my dear stepmother and how she had cared for my hair. I also remembered how, when I was small, I had taken the shears and cut my hair, making bangs for myself.

There were some girls in the room looking on while Effie cut my hair. They told me to look at myself in the mirror which I did. I looked horrible, and I was reminded of how I looked exactly like the Navajo boys and men who had haircuts like mine. Effie asked what I would do with the hair she had cut off, and I said, "I'll keep it for a souvenir." When I told her I looked horrible she said, "Come on, I'm not through; I will make you look like Clara Bow." Clara Bow was the "It Girl" in the 1920s. So Effie curled my hair with an electric hair curler and then put on my forehead what was termed a "spit curl."

It was then time to work in the kitchen--of all places to go with a nice hairdo--and by the time I had finished working in that steaming place my curls had disappeared. From then on I spent my time at night putting my hair up in paper curlers, which was more work than having long hair.

My haircut also lost me a friend, for the head cook, who was almost a mother to me, had advised me against the haircut and the use of makeup. When she could not locate me she yelled out, "Where is Irene?" There I was, sitting right under her nose, peeling potatoes. One girl laughed and said to Mrs. Swingly, "She is right there on the stool, peeling." Mrs. Swingly threw up her hands and said, so everyone could hear, "Irene, you bad girl!" With that she turned away and did not speak to me for almost two weeks. The girls teased me about this.

At the end of my second year at Haskell, four girls returned to the Southwest to go to Albuquerque Indian School. There was room for them because some girls at that school had become delinquent. Two other Navajo girls and I stayed on to finish our four-year terms. I had begun to like Haskell. During my third year I had some new classmates who were very friendly. Also I began to mingle with the high-school students for I was in the ninth grade. I joined the Glee Club and the girls' basketball team. I took a home economics course to fulfill my vocational training requirements. In addition to my classmates, I acquired many friends among other students and among the employees, and I admired the matrons despite their strict attitudes toward us.

During my third and fourth years I tried to acquire everything that is good for a student, and worked hard to get a good report. Before I knew it, the four years were up. I was anxious to go home, and at the same time reluctant to leave Haskell. The school principal urged me to re-enroll, but I was undecided. He said to think it over and send word back as soon as I could.

The bright June Commencement Day for twelfth-grade graduates was inspiring to see. I saw boys and girls I had known for four years graduate from the commercial business course, home economics, nursing, and as bakers. John and George Lini, the great football players, graduated that year. These happy and wonderful memories I took with me back home that summer.

# Chapter 7

# An Indian Student and Her Problems

When Father met me at Fort Defiance, upon my return from Haskell, I hardly knew him. He had taken on years and was old and thin.

Father looked at me for some time. I think he wondered about my bobbed hair and all the new style, perhaps even my actions. I felt out of place again. How these sudden changes make a Navajo student feel is only to be understood by one who has experienced them.

Back in the 1920s and '30s, the returning students' problems were very much unsolved. Unless a Navajo family were well off and could give their children a good home--perhaps some stock and land to start them off--they would in time drift away to nearby towns, or even farther away as I have. Once having left hogan life, and having gotten used to living where there are hygienic facilities, it is very hard to live again in the old hogan way of life. A Navajo boy or girl wants a suitable home, a chance to live the life he has been taught, and an opportunity to find suitable work to support himself and later his family.

The school regime was hard to break away from; it had left me with problems unsolved. I was wholly discouraged and frustrated, so I told Father to leave me at the Fort Defiance school to hunt for work. I did not wish to go home then, but would later in the summer.

I obtained a job doing housework for Mr. Duclos, the Fort Defiance agent, at $30 a month, part of which went back to him for my board. But I was better satisfied there than I would have been sitting around home. At least I was earning money for more education. I worked two months and two weeks; then I visited my father and his family for two weeks.

When I had left the Navajo country years before, I felt heart-break; now I was disappointed in it. I could not make up my mind to stay on the reservation. Hogan life--once a great pleasure to me, and in later years so satisfying--was not for me. I looked forward to the white man's ways and decided to go back to school, this time to Albuquerque Indian School.

Before leaving for Albuquerque, I got sick with tonsilitis. The doctor at Fort Defiance removed my tonsils. I had a hard time recovering. The head nurse thought I should not go back to school because

my system had been poisoned from the bad tonsils. She was afraid that
I might come down with a severe illness which would take my life before
the year was up. But I wouldn't take her advice. Live or die, I was
going back to school.

During that first year at Albuquerque Indian School I kept thinking about what the nurse had said to me. Every time I caught cold I kept
a strict watch over myself. This gave me the idea of taking up practical
nursing at the Indian hospital in Albuquerque as the vocational part of
my training. As at Haskell, part of our training was vocational, part
was academic.

In other respects, Albuquerque Indian School was different from
Haskell, where the students were expected to speak English; at Albuquerque
it seemed that more spoke their native tongue than they did English. In
order to be better equipped to learn, I spoke English with those few who
tried to keep from speaking their native language. The one thing I never
stopped regretting was not having gone back to Haskell to finish high
school. I lost quite a big opportunity by not returning to that fine
school.

In 1928, I switched back to home economics from practical nursing, and in 1929, I received my diploma. During my last years of high
school, a Christian woman encouraged me to take Christian training in
California. This I told her I would do if I could get a summer job with
a good salary. I returned to Fort Defiance and immediately got a job as
a hospital seamstress.

# Chapter 8

## Missionary Zeal

My Christian training began as a small girl when I was sent by Uncle Lewis to learn the Presbyterian teachings. I did not understand all the lessons at that time, but my training was continued at Fort Defiance Boarding School where in later years I felt the missionary zeal.

When I was 14 or 15 years old I attended a two-day Presbyterian conference at Chinle. I went with the Fort Defiance mission interpreter, Mr. Clark, and his wife in their old Model T Ford over the old mountain road. Mrs. Clark was related to my father by clan so she knew me. As we approached Chinle she said, "You will see the Canyon where you were born and raised by your grandmother." When we got to the Rim road she pointed down the huge canyon saying, "There, over around right bend, is where your former home is; some relatives are there now." At Chinle I found that the old trading post I had seen in 1910 was abandoned, and that a mission had been established.

Since I had the good privilege of being taught the Christian way during my childhood at Fort Defiance school, this conference was a wonderful experience for me. I was already caught in the middle between the white man's way and the Navajo way. It was the result of my being kidnapped for education. This I am grateful for.

Years later, in one of my Thanksgiving speeches at our church, I told my people about this gratefulness, and as I did I noticed one old man in the audience nodding his grey head in approval. In a way this happened to be my Christian testimony. I told how Jesus Christ--*Doodaa-Tsaahi*, One Who Never Dies--taught me this way of life so that I am a Christian.

With my mind made up to be a missionary's helper, I took off for Oakland, California, in the fall of 1929, to enter a nine months' Bible study course. As part of my studies, I was sent out to do street work in Berkeley. Mostly I told gospel news to children since I was timid about working on older people. Because I was an Indian, I thought white people all knew more about Christian religion than I did. I enjoyed working with the children.

After finishing the course I stayed on a few more months for additional study. Then I was sent home to work among my people at the

Presbyterian Mission Hospital of Redrock near *Lukachukai*, Arizona.  At that time this place was absolutely isolated.  Mail came in once a week.  There were times when we went without good meals.  It was a lonely experience after tasting the city life, and I wished I were back in California.

My job was to interpret for the pastor at church times; help in the hospital with the patients who were in bed, thus assisting as a practical nurse; and sometimes I helped do the laundry by hand.  There were no laundry facilities.  A Navajo woman did all the laundry by washing in a tub.  Because I worked so hard I lost quite a lot of weight.

Before the year was up the doctor received word to close down the mission for lack of funds.  After the doctor dismissed the patients we packed everything away and cleaned up.  We didn't know whether our checks would come through.  I was receiving $50 a month, part of which went for board.

There was a trading post close to the mission which I think is still operating.  The trader was a friend of mine, and he was glad to see me go because he knew I was not happy there and he thought the job was too hard for a young girl.

When I left I went directly to Gallup, bought a ticket, and left for Oakland.  I was soon back where I wanted to be.  I worked a year for a woman who ran a pawn shop; then I got married to an Oneida boy.

# Chapter 9

## A Broken Marriage and a Family to Support

In olden days, I heard from my elders, marriage to a person from another tribe or to a white person was taboo. If a Navajo married this way he or she would in time get sick and death would result unless the Enemy Way ceremony was performed.

During the first two years of my marriage everything seemed to be all right. Then domestic troubles developed. Oftentimes some Navajo with good intentions would say to me, "You are ailing from *ana'í* (enemy). Why don't you have a squaw dance over you?"

First my husband and I lived in Nevada for a short time; then we went to Tuba City. This was during the great depression years and my husband was always out of a job. As we began to have a family this became most distressing.

My Oneida husband did not like the ways of Navajo life, and I could not help it because I was the product of this life. I guess one might say we married out of our original environments. Without knowing each other's home situations, we had met in the big city and fallen in love.

I soon found out that my husband was far from my ideal. He had a wanderlust, and would go for weeks and months saying he was job hunting but never bringing home the bacon. In time this made me very quarrelsome and irritable, and I put on scenes. After trying to live together for five years, we parted to go our separate ways.

I consider my first marriage a tragedy, a tragedy because there were four small children involved. Untangling this marriage was slow and painful for me. First our separation took place; then years later, with much legal red-tape, I got my divorce.

After our separation I took the boys and began my long struggle for survival. I was ambitious, longing to put the skills I had learned into practice, but in those days it was hard even to get an opportunity to do any kind of work. My uncle George Bancroft, my mother's brother, helped me stay in Tuba City and get work as a field-nurse's helper. This was all-day field work from which I seldom returned before late evening. We took care of a large area including Navajo Mountain, Cow Springs, and

Kayenta. We gave out medicines and treated patients. I never saw a single house, just hogans. I think Uncle George was the only one who had a two-room house near Tuba City.

Many were the times that we got stalled because of car troubles, poor roads, and bad weather. But we managed to get back before morning or start a new work day. Because of these irregular hours, my boss the field nurse got called down by the head doctor at Tuba City. She really told him and the head nurse about the highlights of our hard field trips, and she told them to try it once and find out. She then resigned and I was left without a job after working hard for over a year. I had enjoyed working with the field nurse, and what practical nursing I had learned was used on this job.

I recall one man we attended on our last trip. His name was Navajo Dick. He was laid up with an injured left shoulder which had become swollen and inflamed. The nurse rubbed it with oil and gave him aspirin to relieve the pain. Then we urged him to let us take him in for hospital treatment which he refused. He said he did not care to be in a hospital where so many people died, besides he did not like the food. "I will starve," he said. "I'd rather stay and eat cornmeal food which is more nourishing than hospital food."

Navajo Dick had two wives, and the older one tried her best to make him go with us. I asked him how he got hurt and he said that some policeman from Tuba City had come to arrest him; that he had resisted and got thrown against a post. He was taken into court on charges of witch-crafting, but released due to lack of evidence. Later he developed pneumonia and died at his home.

With my four boys I returned to Chinle to see my father and to look for work. There a man relative who lived in Canyon de Chelly said to me, "You had better file a land claim for the place at Rock Bends Into Water. Your former grandparents and mother lived there many years, so that is yours. By all means get it back for your children. Those people living there do not belong there."

I would not claim the land because the people living there are clan relatives. *Dzaani Łitóli*, the head of the family, is my elder sister in the Navajo way; a distant cousin by the white man's way. She and her family have used the land for farming and grazing, and have built a hogan. They are well established and are making good use of the land. They will use the land as long as they can as *Tótsohnii* Clan. They moved there after Grandmother and my sisters, brothers, and uncles went to Tuba City to make their home with Uncle George who was an interpreter at the agency.

From the time I had learned to write letters, Uncle George Bancroft and I had done a lot of corresponding. Among my keepsakes is the following letter:

Tuba City, Arizona, Jan. 26, 1928

My dear Niece: I do not mean anything to neglect writing all this
length of time. It's just my habit putting off till tomorrow, then
sometime I forget what I had put it off for. I am very proud and
happy over all my little girls doing good at getting an education.
Hoping nothing will happen to interfere as you are going through the
course of your schoolings. And I say, make it good. I don't believe
I will know Adel [a clan relative] when I see her, so tell her to
send me a picture of herself. I haven't seen her since she was a
baby. I like to see my sisters' children all doing well in all their
undertakings. We are all well, that is my family and self, now I
am not doing anything for my living. A man named Frank Walker told
me about your father's brother [Lewis Watchman] being laid off as a
judge for some reason. Little before Christmas we went to Huska's
camp, and spent few days with them. [Huska is my grandmother's
sister's son.] Your sister *Tabah* was with them, she is well, and
has a girl and a boy. I think I will take her to Blue Canyon where
my stocks are running. Your older sister moved to Grey Mountain so
I don't know how she is getting along. Folks all live separate, so
I don't get around much to see them often as I like to. I must stop
here. My love and best wishes to you and Adel.

Your uncle,

George Bancroft


For several years prior to 1928, Uncle George served as a
delegate to the Navajo Tribal Council. That year he quit both his job as
interpreter and his duties as delegate.

My first job at Chinle was doing house work for Mrs. Garcia.
The pay was small but it got us through the winter. Later on I worked at
odd jobs. During this time I moved closer to Chinle School where I am
now living. I started out with a tent house which later I turned into a
shack.

When World War II came I took a job at Bellemont, Arizona,
cleaning the Administration offices. I resigned two years later due to
ill health. Sometime afterwards I went to Flagstaff to seek war work.
I found a job and stayed a year, returning to Chinle several times to
visit my father.

Chapter 10

# The Navajo Way

During all the years I worked and went to school there was little time to live the Navajo way, but I do remember from my childhood experiences the role of the Navajo woman.

The place of a good Navajo woman among her people is one of respect and good influence. Having married and made a home of her own, she is seldom idle. She has her hogan housekeeping to do. As a girl I watched my stepmother do the typical hogan chores, and I learned from her how to keep a hogan clean.

It is customary for the mother or some older woman to get up before sunrise to clean out the ashes and build a fire. If there are goats to milk there is fresh milk for breakfast and, best of all, milk cornmeal cakes. They are like pancakes only lighter and thinner. We ate them without syrup.

After breakfast there was the usual dishwashing and cleaning. The bedding of sheep and goats' skins was shaken and hung out in the fresh air. Not having beds, we slept on the floor upon these skins which are soft and warm. There were no chairs so we sat on the ground.

Women, usually mothers, went to the trading post to do the shopping, but Father did all the buying in our family. When I was little I begged him to bring home some candy, chewing gum, and apples. He always brought some. If we were without money, there were rugs, pelts, wool, and livestock to sell, and silver and turquoise jewelry to pawn.

At harvest time there were bales of hay, dried corn, wheat, canyon peaches (fresh or dried), beans, and melons. There were many acres under cultivation in Canyon de Chelly.

In former years women and girls hunted and picked cactus fruits, yucca bananas, acorns, wild sweet berries, and various kinds of seeds of plants which were roasted and ground into flour. There were wild roots and greens, the latter eaten green or cooked like spinach. There were wild teas which were dried like store tea. There were different kinds of meat: sheep, goat, deer, wild turkey, chicken, prairie dog, squirrel, cattle, and horse. These were cooked fresh or dried for jerky. And in some years there were pinyon nuts; these little nuts are now popular among whites as well as Navajos.

I remember that water and wood were the main things to be provided daily. It was my job to bring water: if nearby I hauled it with buckets; if some distant place, I had the fun of using the burro. One time the burro decided to freshen up by rolling in some ashes. Not having time to get off with the water kegs, I was dumped into the ashes. The water kegs were all right, but I got up looking very much like a clown.

It was also my job to gather wood. In the desert we used greasewood; in the hills and mountains there were plenty of sticks and pieces of wood which did not need chopping. Nowadays the wood is hauled in wagons and trucks.

Navajo women and girls who were weavers worked at their weaving during spare time. I can remember how the Navajo women kept their people alive by weaving rugs and caring for sheep and goats. In this way my stepmother kept us from starving. She wove all the known types of rugs, trading them for food and clothing. She wove for other Navajos who admired her weaving. I can remember how she got 25 goats and sheep by weaving a fine saddle blanket for a rich man with much stock.

My stepmother used to card and spin at night by the light from the wood fire. We did not have kerosene and gasoline lamps until later years.

My father and stepmother got along very well. There were few domestic troubles. Having regarded poverty as a natural condition of life, my parents and sisters shared happily the meager supplies we had. Food, clothes, and shelter we had. These were the most important, and the most needed.

My stepmother made the most of whatever we had. She cooked the Navajo way, and was a good cook. I loved her bread stuffs of store flour and Indian cornmeal. She made fried bread and plain tortillas cooked on a hot stone griddle or on a wire roaster. She made cornbread out of fresh corn and dried cornmeal and cooked it in cornhusks, some plain and some sweetened. She made biscuits out of flour and baked them upon hot ashes covered with a skillet. This was what I liked best of all, especially when there was mutton stew to go with them. I have learned these recipes and how to cook them the Navajo way.

When my stepmother was busy or ill I did the baby-sitting for her. I would take the baby on my back and go for a stroll.

Navajo mothers train their children at an early age to respect their elders; to learn the clan traditions; to be industrious, not lazy and slothful; to be honest, not rowdy. When old enough they are taught the moral lessons. During my girlhood my father saw to it that I stayed home when there was a ceremonial or dance going on nearby, especially a squaw dance. He said he just did not want to see me chase and grab boys and men to dance with.

When Navajo children get out of control, various methods are used to check them. One way is to throw cold water on them, enough to arouse them out of naughtiness. Sparing the rod, a light whipping or a paddling with a stick is usually sufficient. Also, false warnings are used such as: "The cow will hear you crying and butt you with those sharp horns," or "Your grandfather will whip you; he has a whip that stings to use on naughty children," or if it is at night, "The owl is out; he is hooting; listen." If some person is feared, his characteristics or disfiguring marks are mentioned to the child who is told, "So and so will come and check on you if you are naughty." When I was small I cried a lot, so I was told that if I didn't stop crying, "*Chadi* will come and get you." *Chadi* was a man with no lower lip. He wore a cloth over that part of his face and I was afraid of him.

I have mentioned that my father disapproved of my going to squaw dances. The squaw-dance method of selecting a partner is to look around for males not of your clan relations. When a girl doesn't know whom to choose, she can get advice from a chaperone, usually her mother. Then the girl stalks the man or boy through the crowd and grabs him. If the girl is shy her chaperone will help her. The man or boy usually pays the girl in dimes or quarters. Father said dancing would make me become pleasure hunting and forget my home and duties. Worse yet, I might become a loose woman, an *ałjiłnii*.

Father didn't allow us girls to go to towns or to hang around trading posts for fear that we would become *Kin yąąh sizíinii* (She Who Stands Beside the House). Little girls are trained to be modest. They wear long skirts and blouses to cover their bodies, and sit like their mothers--not like boys and men. They are told not to play with boys too much, and to keep their distance with brothers and near cousins.

I have mentioned those responsibilities and duties of a good Navajo woman. Undoubtedly they implanted enduring love and respect toward parents who loved and cared for them. So it was with me toward my father who was a mother to me after Mother died. To me my father was a fine man, always looking after my welfare. He was a hard worker. Although I spent only three months out of the year with him, his teaching and his encouragement to learn all I could at school have never been forgotten. Always I thought of him first when I felt discouraged and helpless. During my childhood days I feared losing my father. Perhaps this was due to losing my mother when I needed her most. Having had the heartbreaking experience of being without a mother, I did not want Father to die and leave me alone.

# Chapter 11

# My Father

Father was a small-time medicine man.  He knew the Devil
Chasing Ceremony and also a bit of the Water Chant.  In his youth he
herded sheep for his father and mother.  He had a large flock of his own,
and after he married Mother he gave her part of the sheep and goats; what
was left he gambled away.

Father told me about his gambling days in Canyon de Chelly.
He said:

There were times when police raids occurred.  Once I was arrested
with some men and taken to Fort Defiance where I was sentenced for
a good length of time.  I was confined all winter and early spring.
While the ice was thick I planted trees on the school campus.  Chopping through ice was a very hard and freezing job.  There were eight
of us jailed.  Each day we were taken out of the old jail house,
which at that time was a brand new one over across the wash.
    I lost everything because an old Navajo man put a curse on me,
saying, "You, Son of Watchman, you think you can ridicule me and
get by with it.  Well, you have gambled long enough, cheating and
taking my grandson's silver buttons.  You will lose everything and
die chewing on the soles of your moccasins."

After Father lost everything he went away to work on the railroad with his brother Lewis.  They worked around Denver, Chicago, and in
the East where he got hurt handling heavy equipment.  Father said, "I
was laid up for six months in hospital in New York City.  The hospital
was big and strange.  The doctors were kind to me and the nurses, too.
Besides giving me medicine they fed me plenty of good food, large steaks
and all kinds of good vegetables.  I think the vegetables healed me."

My father learned to build stone houses.  In this way he sup-
ported us.  Also he worked as a blacksmith, sharpening tools for the coal
miners around Gallup.  We were always moving around because of his work.
He never saved like Uncle Lewis did.

With my stepmother Father acquired a few sheep and goats.  This
was before permit days.  Afterwards, like many other small owners, they
lost out while the large owners got around the government, and in some
cases even managed to increase their herds.  It should be explained that

because of over-grazing on the reservation, it was necessary in the 1930s to limit the number of sheep so as to reduce erosion and grass shortage. All this caused much confusion and many Navajos sold below their quotas, and others who had few sheep ended up with even fewer. My father ended up with none at all.

In the spring of 1944, Father fell from a tree. When I saw him after the accident he was lying on a stretcher, unable to move his lower limbs. Despite the seriousness of his injury I ordered a pair of crutches for him, for I was in hopes that he would soon be healed.

At the end of four months he wasn't any better. I visited him several times from Flagstaff where I was working. During my last visit he told me he was all right and not to worry. I planned to return within two weeks.

I have heard about people seeing apparitions or ghosts. This happened to me in the early hours of the morning at the exact time my father passed away. He appeared in my sleep just as healthy and well. His body radiated with light as he stood before me. He then plainly said, "I am healed, my child." I woke and found it to be a dream. When I told my family about it, I remarked that I would leave on Friday evening to visit him. I was very happy and told everyone I knew about his being healed. Just as I was about to leave for the reservation I got a letter from a relative telling me of Father's death and burial. With much sadness I visited his grave. My stepmother said that she, too, had written me, but I never received her letter. Both of us grieved for many years.

Father passed away five months after his injury. He was 87 years old, and I had lost him before I was half his age. He was a strong healthy man when he broke his hip. It happened while he was chopping off branches for a shade house for his family. Greyeyes said, "He would have died of old age if he didn't fall off the tree."

# Chapter 12

## Greyeyes

During my girlhood days there was an old white man, a fortune teller, who worked at Fort Defiance. After hearing him read the palms of several girls, I held out my hand to him. He looked me over and said," You have a long life to live and this means you will become an old lady. You will marry but it will not be a good one. You will have plenty of trouble. Cheer up, you will have four boys and I see one will be a great man, maybe the President of the USA. You will recover from a terrible illness, and live a nice life to your old age. Also you will marry again, this time to an old man."

How the girls giggled at this, but I was floored. I said, "Oh no, Mr. Shinn!" He said, "But he will take care of you and be good to you. After all you will be happy and have a good home."

In the year of 1942, Greyeyes and I were joined by common-law marriage. Greyeyes was 20 years older than I; he had been married three times before and had daughters and sons.

Joining ourselves in common-law marriage was like this: my husband said that his folks told him, "There she is in Chinle with four boys, no husband. She needs a man and you need a wife instead of getting old by yourself and staying at your mother's home. It would be a good idea to get together." So he asked if I would let him be my helpmate, and I agreed.

My sister *Ałnááyiibah* helped out on this marriage as my father was rather reluctant about it. Later we had a church marriage performed by Reverend Grey of Trinity Presbyterian as common-law marriage became illegal on the reservation around 1945.

When I was a little girl Greyeyes was married to one of my close cousins, a clan sister through an aunt. I used to think he was my brother so I called him *shinaaí* (my older brother). He was very thoughtful and nice and I got quite attached to him. When we went on long journeys he carried me on his back. I grew to expect this whenever we went somewhere, and once demanded that he carry me. His wife said, "Get busy and do as she says; she may become your wife someday." After our marriage Greyeyes said, "This was just a joke for me then, but how our destinies work out--unavoidable for both of us; how I appreciate living just like this, well satisfied just living a Navajo life—an age life."

Greyeyes is a narrator of Navajo ways in stories and chants. Evening comes and long into the night we exchange yarns. He does all the chanting and story-telling until I fall asleep. During my illnesses this has been the source of a happy feeling, a quiet affirmation. Married life with Greyeyes has been good.

Many are the stories Greyeyes has told me about his young days. One I remember is how the boys were made to rise before sunrise and race; in winter they rolled in the snow. This was to make them strong, live longer, and endure hardships.

Some girls were made to do the same things as the boys. Greyeyes's mother was raised this way. She was a tomboy type, and always wanted to outdo the boys at play or work. She learned to tame and handle horses. By doing these hard things she acquired a fine physique and plenty of vitality. She had masculine strength in her middle age. I remember how she grabbed a horse by the bridle, pulled the man out of the saddle, and took his groceries away—all because he had made fun of her in-laws. The Navajo have a custom of fun making, jesting with each other about cousins and in-laws; this makes for grabbing of property and tearing of clothes.

Greyeyes's family are hard-working, traditional Navajos. They believe in the Navajo religion, which they often use for sickness, bad dreams, prosperity, and well being. They own sheep and goats and the women are good weavers of rugs.

Greyeyes was born in Canyon de Chelly about 82 years ago. His father, *Hastiin Danahalstui*, married his mother when she was a young girl. Greyeyes was the firstborn of six children. His father left his mother and married a young girl cousin. His mother then married Limpy of Canyon del Muerto, by whom she had two boys.

Greyeyes was raised like the typical Navajo of his time. He never attended school. He was taught stock raising and how to be a medicine man. He learned *Hózhǫ́ǫ́jí* songs and prayers, *Yeibichai* songs, the War Dance and the Squaw Dance, and even a little about the Devil Chasing Ceremony, one of the oldest Navajo religious ceremonies.

When Greyeyes was about 38 years of age he had trouble with a government officer on the reservation. I don't recall what position this man held, but it appeared that he was an acting officer of the Navajo police force. At that time some of the Navajos were beginning to drink intoxicating liquor and a few of them obtained it from Gallup to bootleg to their people.

The incident happened early in the fall of 1923. Greyeyes had taken his family to a Fire Dance near Red Lake, now called Navajo. Early in the morning following the dance, Greyeyes packed his wagon and left for home with his wife and their baby boy, who was in a cradle. They had not gone far before this white officer and three Navajo policemen caught up with them. They were ordered to stop and be searched for the liquor they were reported to have bootlegged at the Fire Dance.

Greyeyes told them he was not guilty of the charge and remained sitting in the wagon. The wagon was then searched and bedding, grub (including a bag of boiled mutton), and some soda pop were thrown out. Then Greyeyes's wife was forced out of the wagon and the baby boy set roughly on the ground. The white officer grabbed Greyeyes and the struggle began. Greyeyes said, "I was already mad at him for the way my property was searched and I lost my temper. I hit him and knocked him down. Then I took out my pistol and shot him in the neck. When I saw what I had done I looked at the Navajo officers; they were so shocked they stood stupified for some minutes; then all ran for cover."

Greyeyes took one horse, told his wife he was heading home to his mother in Canyon de Chelly, and took off. He was in hiding for some time while the US sheriffs were looking for him. They went to Cozy McSparron's Trading Post in Chinle. Cozy McSparron and other Anglo friends were shocked, but they agreed to help Greyeyes if he would give himself up. One of Greyeyes's brothers acted as a go-between.

Greyeyes was arrested and taken to St. Johns, then to Prescott. After many days he was sentenced to serve a term for manslaughter. Greyeyes's friends, both Anglo and Navajo, raised funds for his lawyer.

The man Greyeyes shot was nicknamed Gopher because he was very overbearing and did things to Navajos by threats. Greyeyes said, "Every Navajo and non-Navajo who knew that man I shot, knows the kind of man he was."

Greyeyes was one of the first entertainers for the Gallup Ceremonials. His talents as a baritone singer caught the attention of his white friends, Mike Kirk, Cozy McSparron, and Howard Wilson, who trained and directed him. Greyeyes told me that he sang and danced for audiences in Santa Fe, Albuquerque, Phoenix, and Denver. He also played the roles of spy and guide for movie people. I remember one picture called *Colorado Territory* made by Warner Brothers.

Greyeyes loves horses. He claims they are more useful than cattle, sheep, or goats. He had one horse tamed for all-around use. It got in the habit of trespassing on the government school grounds where there was blue grass, and also some garden plots belonging to the employees. Two of them filed complaints with the Tribal Council and my husband was required to serve 24 hours in jail for this. Later on some cattle guards were installed at the grounds but Sputnik, the name given him by my boys, managed to get in somehow.

After that my husband sold him to a Hopi Indian who lived some distance from Chinle. A few days afterward the Hopi was back to inform my husband that Sputnik had run away from his son and he had found him half-way back to Chinle.

Greyeyes has a permit for five horses and five sheep units. He gave me a young mare and from her I got some fine Appaloosas which I sold. All my mother's goats and a few sheep were assigned me when I was small but these were taken away by the other folks when they moved to Tuba City. A burro which my father had given me died when I was at Haskell. I have a land-use permit, issued by the Bureau of Indian Affairs, for the five acres on which Greyeyes and I live. My youngest son will take this over someday.

# Chapter 13

## Religious Beliefs and Practices

My introduction to the Peyote Cult, though I did not know it at the time, was years ago when it was my job to keep a fire going at night for two old men, *Dághá Sikaad* (Spread Out Mustache) and *Hastiin Sisíi'ii* (The Numb One). Their prediction was that *Dine'é* would some-day adopt a new religion. It was said that this religion, which is from enemy people's culture, mixed Indian and white, would bring about con-fusion among *Dine'é*. It first appeared among the Utes, and our people living near them took a taste. From there it spread throughout the reserva-tion, even into the Tribal Council at Window Rock where it caused more con-fusion because some people who used peyote had control of the council. In our Chinle chapter there were persons who upheld these councilmen, speak-ing in favor of freedom of worship. If our people continue to use this peyote stuff they will lose modesty in both morals and ambition.

When our great *Hózhǫǫjí* Way is not being used anymore, *Sa'a Naagháii* will take it away from us forever. Our people no longer observe even the smallest beliefs, such as daily rituals by which all the hogan tasks and habitual ways were done. I recall how the women got up before sunrise and took out the ashes, saying a prayer as they did so. When they finished cooking, the charcoal was poked back into the fire with a prayer of gratitude and abundant blessings were asked that all the household members would walk the Blessing Way.

Stirring sticks used to stir mush were objects of prayers; each time they were used the user offered up a prayer. Even children were taught rituals. When a child lost a milk tooth he ran outside with it, closed his eyes, turned his face away and threw the tooth over his right shoulder toward the east with these words, "May I eat a fat gopher with the new one." This was done so he would grow a strong tooth that would last to old age.

In early times *Dine'é* were very religious; they were zealous with all their rituals. They went out before sunrise with their pollen to pray, especially after a bad dream.

*Dine'é* religion is for healing the sick of body and mind. In-tricate chants to drive out evil spirits and resist witches and ghosts, numerous sandpaintings, prayers, and blessings to please the gods—all these are part of the ritual for the many different ceremonies that make

51

up the *Hózhǫ́ǫ́jí* Way.

The People believe in one great divine supreme being and in a good universe, so *Dine'é* want to live a good life. They also believe there are forms of witchcraft and sorcery. These were very much in use during primitive days but are now almost stamped out, though one still hears rumors about witchcraft.

*Dine'é* religion is big, filled with reverence for the great spirit who has control over all. *Dine'é* found everlasting peace in some things they did; their findings confirmed their customs. So we should say little or nothing against their religion. Many present-day medicine men practice the ceremonies to heal those sick in body and mind. To me it is like having first the light of fire, then the candle, oil, gas, and finally electricity to shed an even broader light.

Long ago *Dine'é* learned to associate material beauty with the beauty of holiness. Their prayer for this is:

White Shell Woman, Changing Woman, Mother Earth, Father Sky, ever-
    lasting and peaceful,
Turquoise Woman, Changing Woman, everlasting and peaceful,
With beauty before me I walk
With beauty behind me I walk
With beauty above me I walk
With beauty under me I walk
With beauty beside me I walk.

When the early missionaries came upon *Dine'é* they found a re-ligion already operating. They directed this religion into the Christian way. I was diverted from my traditional religion through education. I was taught Christianity, learned and accepted it. I consider myself born into a new way of life--the God way, or as a Navajo would say, *Oodláanii*, or believer.

I am asked when I am ill, "Why do you not have a medicine man sing over you?" Then, if another person is present, she is likely to say, "Oh, Irene is one of those Short Coats." Short Coats are Protestants; Long Coats are Catholics. Usually these remarks are meant as criticisms.

Several times my husband has persuaded me to have a sing over me, twice the Blessing Way: one after my operation; one because a mouse chewed on my clothes. Now I am constantly in ill health and Greyeyes says I ought to have a four-day sing pertaining to lightning and water, the Shooting Way (female) rite, Feather Chant. But I have declined because of heavy expenses and the amount of work involved for the family. Also, it would be a strain on me, and besides I have given myself to the Christian way.

When our Blessing Way is forgotten, our elders say the earth will be destroyed by fire. Already, in these days, our medicine men do not know the correct procedures for our ceremonies. Of the 50 or more of our big and little ceremonies, many have been forgotten. Now we know the few that can be remembered, but they are not performed skillfully the way they were by the old-time medicine men.

These days some of our medicine men have become unscrupulous; they have cast off some of the ancient beliefs and are using parts of the ceremonies for public shows to gain profits instead of for healing purposes. Our elders used to say, "There will come a time when The People will desert the old ways." It was said that women and girls would wear trousers instead of skirts, bob hair, pluck eyebrows, wear red stuff on their lips. That time is here. I see it all around.

Chapter 14

# Political Systems, Old and New

In the beginning, Greyeyes said, the Navajo people knew nothing of having one chief or leader for the whole tribe. They were a wandering people who moved in groups, usually clan groups. They had leaders--war chiefs to lead them when they were attacked by enemies; peace chiefs, who were orators, to look after their welfare and give advice and instruction. This is the way it was when our people were captured and taken away in 1863.

Greyeyes said that while the Navajos were prisoners-of-war at Fort Sumner they led miserable lives. Because they were costing the government so much money, it was decided that they should be transferred to Indian territory in Oklahoma. When it was time for them to leave they put up an uproar, especially the women. They begged the colonel in charge to let them return to their own country. The colonel wanted to know what was so fine about their country since there was nothing there to offer them a good living. He said they would only kill, make war, and steal when they got back. The Navajos said, "No, we will be good. We have learned not to carry on war and steal and kill. And there will be plenty of wild food such as pinyon nuts, fruit, and game to live on." Then one old woman cried out, "Please, my son, let us go. I am lonesome for my land, my dear Chinle and Canyon de Chelly."

The colonel softened and said he would try to get the President's permission. As a result, a treaty was made in 1868 which allowed the Navajos to return to their homeland after five years of captivity. Under the treaty they faced a new way of living, the white man's way. This meant an end to a governmental system under war chiefs and peace chiefs, and the beginning of having one head-man with his helpers.

Early in the 1900s the reservation was divided into five districts, each with a representative to meet with government officials at Fort Defiance. Later on, after the discovery of coal, gas, oil, and other natural resources, it was necessary to have full-time officials to look after the tribe's business, so the Navajos elected a chairman, vice-chairman, secretary, and treasurer. The big central meeting place was moved to Window Rock.

To give the Navajos more voice in governmental affairs, Indian agent John Hunter, in 1923 or 1924, suggested they organize local chapters to discuss local problems and needs, such as getting more and better schools and starting land improvement projects. This idea was developed further by a white-haired man named Hagerman who went among the Navajos to assist them in using the governmental process. The chapters, which became the grass roots of the Tribal Council, functioned effectively, and many Navajos assumed positions of authority in both the council and the chapters, some doing good jobs, others not.

Thus the Navajos began their great business with people from the outside world, as well as taking care of local problems such as lawlessness and disputes over land.

I had no thought of getting involved in local chapter activities in Chinle where I lived, but in 1948 it came about in this way. Upon my husband's return from a sing ceremony he said, "People are disturbed by a crooked deal done by the chapter officials. This deal was done last spring."

I expressed my total ignorance as to what was going on within the chapter. Greyeyes explained that the deal had been made without calling a meeting. He said:

> The chapter officers took out the money--$200 from one trading post where it had been deposited by a movie company--which was for the people of Canyon de Chelly to use for some good. Now the Chinle delegate has put in his resignation and we must elect someone to serve the rest of his unfinished term. When the election of the new delegate comes about, the people who do not like this deal are planning to recall the chapter officers and elect new ones, and they are going to find out what really has been done with the $200 that has been taken out of deposit.

The day of the meeting came. My half sister Ałnááyibah and her mother urged me to go with them to vote for Joe Carroll.

The meeting place was half full when we got there; later it filled up and people stood outside. The district supervisor from the Bureau of Indian Affairs was there, sitting with the old officers. At this time it was customary for the Bureau to supervise chapter meetings.

After the meeting was opened, the supervisor read the resignation of the delegate due to illness. Three nominations for a new delegate were then made, with Joe Carroll receiving a majority of the votes. He took the floor to accept the office, and followed with a protest about the deal the chapter officers had made. This caused a lot of commotion and many questions were directed to the officers who defended themselves by saying that the district supervisor had permitted the action. The money had been used for hay which the trader sold to the people so they could work on their irrigation ditches and farm land. However, most of the farms were in the Cottonwood area, and some were near the Valley store. The Canyon people, for whom the money had been deposited, did not get a cent.

The protests became so hot that the officers got angry and said they would not hold office any longer. They felt they were not appreciated, that they had been unduly criticized, and that being officers was a waste of time which took energy but gave them no pay for their work.

The district supervisor then asked the participants to put forward a motion to carry on a new election of chapter officers if that was what they desired. The motion carried with little opposition. Thomas Attison was elected chairman and Harry Price vice-chairman. When it came to electing a secretary, Joe Carroll made the nomination by saying, "Now I wish to nominate a lady as our chapter secretary. We have never had a lady officer; this will be the first time. I think she can handle the work very well. I nominate Irene Stewart, Greyeyes's wife." The motion was seconded by Blue Eyes, a Navajo from Canyon de Chelly, now deceased. Other nominees were called for; there being none, the vote was taken. A majority stood up; only seven were opposed.

The district supervisor called the newly elected officers to take their places as the old officers left. Each new officer gave a speech. I remember the vice-chairman saying, "We intend to sweep out at Window Rock even as we did here. There are people with snatching claws holding office." Sad to say, he dropped out after meeting with us only six months. This continued to happen with our chairmen and vice-chairmen as the years went by. Only delegate Joe Carroll and I stayed on. Each time there was an election we were returned to office, Joe serving 16 years. I served almost 15 years, dropping out only because of a prolonged illness.

In the Tribal Council election of 1955, I was one of three candidates for delegate in Chinle, running against two capable men. My supporters told me I must make campaign speeches in the Chinle chapter area. I had gotten used to writing speeches for others, but had no experience in making them. During one of my discouraged moments over this problem I met Annie Wauneka, the only woman council member at that time. When we got around to talking about the election, I told her I felt that I would lose. She said, "Oh, come on, don't talk like that; do your best and make up your mind to win. I want you to win over the two men and be with me in the council meetings. We'll join up and really work; there is plenty to do. We will go places together, so work hard. It is not hard at all when you really put all you've got into it. You've had more education than I've had."

I told Annie how I had been publicly accused of being a politician. She said, "That is all right. You are doing just that right now— talking, talking about people and community problems. Election time is a good time to show it up."

I lost in the final vote for delegate in Chinle. Joe Carroll was reelected. I continued on with my job as secretary, running again for delegate in 1959. I was one of five nominees, but lost out on the first vote for candidates. In 1963, my illness forced me to resign from my chapter duties.

These days I see more young Navajo girls and women serving as chapter officers. Possibly some of them will be elected councilmen. It would not be surprising to see a woman as chairman of the Tribal Council.

I remember back in 1926 when a Navajo woman was elected secretary to the Tribal Council. She wore primitive clothes, her hair tied in the traditional knot. After being elected she walked up to the front and took a seat with Henry Taliman, chairman, and Deshney, vice-chairman. I was very much interested in her, watching her all the while during the meetings. She did not take notes of the meetings; she just sat and listened to the discussion and the talks. In those days the council met in the old school auditorium. On fine summer and early fall days they met on the campus lawn.

Now the council has expanded in every way, functioning with much dignity and authority. The council delegates, chapter officers, and tribal officers and employees make a big thing of it at Window Rock, and back home they make things move along. In my experience the chapter secretary has the hardest job, does all the work that needs to be carried on for the community, and also sees to the welfare of the people.

As secretary I have met up with some unpleasant circumstances. I have had to bear a lot of cutting and harsh criticism from other chapter members, tribal employees, and persons connected with the Navajos. But there were always those with understanding and unprejudiced minds who helped me carry on my work, especially my Chinle chapter supporters. To them my gratefulness is due. Now, when they meet me, they say, "Irene, when shall we hoe and pull weeds again?"

# Chapter 15

## Duties and Experiences as Chapter Secretary

As secretary of the Chinle chapter it was my duty to conform to chapter rules and policies, record the minutes of the meetings, and take them to the district office. The supervisor then took under consideration the matters voted on at the meetings which included such requests as a chapter house, a general hospital, a jail with a local court, a bridge across Chinle Wash, a bigger school, and the removal of the airport to a distant location to avoid plane crashes in residential areas.

I have stated that the secretary's job is about the hardest. All who have had a part in this will agree with me, for the job is very complicated. It encompasses all discussions of tribal matters on state, county, and local levels, as well as problems affecting the welfare of individuals and the community. The job took a lot of time and thinking on my part.

Oftentimes chapter meetings become very tedious, with long drawn-out talks of the old ways, how old leaders used to conduct meetings, give talks, and control the people, and how we must abide by the old treaties as well as the new regulations and laws from the Department of the Interior and its Bureau of Indian Affairs.

Then there were the unpleasant experiences such as being awakened by a police officer and handed a subpoena to appear in St. Johns' court to be a witness in a political matter. It had to do with a young uneducated Navajo, a veteran of World War II, who had registered to vote in the 1956 election. He maintained he had a right to vote because he was a veteran, but Arizona law said he was ineligible because he was uneducated and illiterate. As registrar for the Chinle precinct that year, I was called to the witness stand to testify. I was never advised as to the outcome of the case.

Another experience I had involved an aggressive and unpopular policeman who was carrying on an adulterous affair. The chapter held a meeting, discussed his behavior, and voted for his removal. A petition was filed and over 100 names secured. This was sent to headquarters and the chief of police, a white man, was sent out to handle the case. For some reason, the woman in this adultery case filed a complaint against the policeman which turned the matter into a court affair.

59

Reports that the policeman was being allowed to resign to escape being fired reached us the day before the court met. An arrangement with one of the judges who lived nearby had been made in order that the policeman's resignation could be made a matter of record. When we met the following morning, the chief of police advised us that the policeman had resigned the preceding night at 10 o'clock at a certain judge's home, that there was no room for us to bring our complaint or to get him fired, that the petition was worthless and of no use, and that if he wanted to he could have jailed the writer for libel.

When court adjourned I could not remain silent, for I had written up the petition for the people who had brought their complaints to the chapter. I told the chief of police it was my duty, by majority vote, to write up the petition and if he wanted to jail me he should jail all the petitioners. My husband then joined me, roaring out that this was a crooked deal. This aroused the people standing nearby, and they rallied around us.

The chief of police took us before the district supervisor who gave orders that we were not to interfere with court decisions. We were told that if court were still in session, we would be arrested for contempt of court. He said this was a warning not to cause further confusion at court hearings. The chief of police then reminded my husband that he had had a bad record in the past and could be arrested for breaking his probation pledge. To further scare us, we were told that a bad report would be filed against us and kept in the office.

After being excused we walked quite a distance from the scene, only to be overtaken by the chief of police. He said that the district supervisor told him that we were committing adultery by living together without a marriage certificate, and if this were true we were under arrest. I said we had been joined in common-law marriage according to tribal custom in 1942, two years or more before the new marriage law had gone into effect. He acknowledged that this was so, but said to be sure and get a marriage certificate before very long, or else. Then he let us go.

Another unpleasant experience centered around a forged check. We had $725 in the Merchants Bank in Gallup, and all bills paid, when a new chairman took over. During the fourth month of his term, I received a cancelled check for $250, written out to Mathews Furniture Company of Gallup and carrying the names of Walker Norcross and Irene Stewart as signers. I was flabbergasted because I had never signed my name to it, nor did I have any knowledge of the purchase for which it was meant. I contacted Mr. Mathews, his bank, and the vice-chairman of our chapter, none of whom were able to trace down the check. Mr. Mathews told me that a man had called him by telephone saying that the chapter was putting on a bingo party and needed some things. The man said he was sending somebody to pick up the stuff which, as it turned out, included some men's clothing and a request for $50 in cash. We were, of course, reimbursed for the full amount of the check.

While I was secretary there were many complaints and protests over the holding of chapter dances, which have continued to this day.

60

Some said dances should not be allowed in chapter houses because youths stayed out all night when they were held, and then missed the squaw dances three nights in a row. They said they could not discipline these youths because of the dances. I felt these youths were not all bad, and could be disciplined. During the dances and at other chapter activities, the majority of them behaved and did not indulge in misdemeanors. Also, these dances and other activities brought in money to operate the chapter house.

Whenever there were difficulties some were quick to criticize. One man said, "We should not allow women to take office in our Tribal Council and chapters. Look at the situation in Chinle now: dances, dances here and there; we ought not allow dances in the chapter houses." One woman suggested that the chapter house be closed down because of the late activities which kept youths out at night.

The Navajo have a legend about a woman leader. Her name was *Asdzą́ą́ Naat'áani* (Woman Chief). She was the queen of her people in the underworld before the Navajos came to this land. Her authority was mostly over women and girls. She became lax in her authority, especially in regard to moral principles, thus making it easy for other women to become loose in their morals. Even her daughter was unfaithful to her husband.

There were many quarrels between the men and the women over who was to support whom. The women said they did not need men to support them, and this made the men angry. They decided to leave the women all to themselves and to make a new home far across a big sea.

In time, life became hard for both sexes but the queen and her daughter remained stubborn and would do nothing to bring the sexes back together. Finally, after four years, an old wise owl advised them there would be no more *Dine'é* if they continued with their foolishness. This made them admit that they were wrong, and ever since the men have taken over as rulers.

My people have this story in mind when they criticize a woman leader. They say there will be confusion within the tribe whenever a Navajo woman takes office.

During the early years of my service in the Chinle chapter, we did not have our own place to meet. We met in government buildings, usually a school room or the old auditorium. When these places were occupied or closed to us for some reason, we met out in the open. Many were the times when I held meetings at the Garcia trading post.

I urged the people to plan for a place of our own where we could hold our much-needed meetings. We asked for an old abandoned trading post which belonged to one of the traders, and were told that we could have the old adobe bricks and logs. We were in the process of completing one large room when the Tribal Council gave us funds for a new chapter house.

When I first became chapter secretary there was no pay for officers. After about five or six years, the Tribal Council recognized the

chapters as an essential part of the tribe's government and granted officers $12 for each meeting.  This made us much more secure and gave us
a feeling of importance.  Now the pay has gone up to $20 per meeting.

Chapter 16

# Arbitration Cases

Aside from the activities already mentioned, chapter officers are arbiters. The judge turned over to us the cases he thought could be ironed out and settled out of court. We handled a few such cases each year. Some cases were brought directly to us, notifying us in advance of the time and place to conduct the discussion and arrange for the settlement. In only a few cases were we unable to bring about agreement and save the parties from going to court. We handled a rape case, friction with police, domestic problems, property disputes, stock problems, and witchcraft accusations.

The rape case was in 1961 in the Valley store section. The mother said her daughter told her that she had been raped by her brother-in-law. The family of the girl knew rape was a federal crime but wanted to take the matter up first with the chapter officers. The chairman and the vice-chairman questioned the man and the girl as to how it all happened. The girl said she had been attacked; the man denied it, saying that the girl had initiated the action and that he had not forced her.

The girl was then asked why she reported the matter to her mother, and she answered, "I was afraid I might have a baby without a father." The vice-chairman asked where it had happened, and she said, "It happened in my mother's hogan. He came around when my mother and father were away. He asked for a drink of water which I gave him."

The chairman said, "This is a hard case for us. It should be reported to the authorities. Also, a doctor's examination is needed in such cases." Then he said, "How old are you?"
The girl answered, "I am 20 years old."
"Well," said the chairman, "you are old enough to protect yourself. Why did you allow him to come in when you were alone?"
"The girl answered, "I didn't allow him; he just came in and asked for a drink of water."
The chairman asked, "Was he intoxicated; did he smell of liquor?"
The girl answered, "No, he did not appear drunk nor smell so."
The man then spoke up, saying, "She did not even fight me."
"This sounds like you liked each other," said the chairman. "You are 20 years old; over 18 you are to make your own decisions. So think about it, and if you wish to press charges yourself, do so. If he is found guilty he will be sentenced to jail--penitentiary in some far-off

place for many years. This kind of rape case is entirely out of our hands. We have been called in to discuss this matter with you and we feel we've done so. The secretary will put in a written report on this if you bring it to court, and we will probably be at the hearing."

The meeting was adjourned at 11:15 p.m. Some time passed before we heard anything further about this case. We were told that the family of the man wanted the matter dropped because the 20-year-old girl was sort of a loose type anyway. Nothing further was reported to us.

The next case is about a common-law marriage. A young man lived with a girl and they had a baby boy. At first they lived together happily, but then they quarreled and had a fight. The girl took the baby to her mother's home and stayed. Then the mother of the young man called us to take up the problem and get the girl back to him. We met together at the girl's mother's hogan where we discussed the situation. The young man's mother begged that the girl and baby be allowed to return to them.

The girl's father and mother were opposed, especially the father because he didn't want his daughter to live in common-law marriage. "In the first place," he said, "my daughter went to Chinle to work and got into this kind of marriage without notifying us, her parents. So it is not my intention to go lightly on the matter. I want to have a thorough discussion with other authorities I have in mind. They are the delegate and community officer of *Nazlini* Chapter. Furthermore, this boy is too irresponsible to have a wife and family."

The Chinle delegate and the two chapter officers did their utmost to bring about good feelings and some sort of favorable agreement, but the father of the girl went outside and refused to come back. We adjourned the meeting.

Later the *Nazlini* Chapter officers and delegate called the Chinle officers and settled the problem for the families. The couple got a Christian marriage in one of the churches here. Now they have a large family, land, and a good home.

A rather unusual matter which we handled at the judge's request involved three under-age girls. Their mother was dead, and their father paid little attention to their needs--perhaps because he was ill most of the time. These three beautiful girls were loose, drank, stayed up all night in the company of boys and even married men, and they did not attend school.

One of the girls and an older woman who was her aunt were out one night with two married men. The aunt left with her friend, leaving the girl alone with a man who was said to have grabbed her. She got away and reported what had happened to her uncle and father the next day. Since the girl was under age, a relative filed a complaint against the man, and this is what brought the matter before the court.

We learned that the man was drunk, but also that this girl and her two sisters were delinquent. We decided they needed better care and should be going to school. The outcome was that they were sent away to Intermountain Indian School in Utah.

Now the girls are married properly and have families. One of them thanked me, saying, "Irene, I am glad and thankful about what you have done for me and my two sisters."

There was one case involving an elderly couple who were having marital troubles. The wife complained of cruelty and non-support. The old man had run her out and she was staying with one of her married daughters. She wanted to file for a divorce, but her sons and daughters were opposed to such an action, so she called us to meet with them at the home of the old man.

The old man was very stubborn. He said, "I will not take any counsel from the delegate or the chapter officers. But I will listen to one man, that old man Greyeyes."

We went and got my husband, and when he sat down near the old man they exchanged clanship greetings. Then cheerful greetings were exchanged all around. Since the woman was related to my husband, the old man backed down from his stubborn position, and was ready to discuss the problem.

But first we were given food before the long tiresome talks, criticisms, and blaming-the-other-fellow began. Then each attacked the other as to why they could not live agreeably. Finally, after three or four hours, we got the old people to abandon their rash plan for divorce.

During the discussion it developed that the old man was jealous because his wife talked so much to a man in their neighborhood. My husband said, "Treat your wife like I treat my young wife or you will lose her. I should miss you as my dear old longtime in-law if your wife divorces you." Then the chapter officers joined in with instructions and the old man melted down and promised he would not cause any more quarrels.

Other disputes we settled involved farm land, grazing rights, and fencing areas. After the grazing committees were organized, chapter officers no longer had jurisdiction over these matters.

On one occasion, the officers of our chapter were called upon to witness and give instructions to the bride and groom at the traditional basket-ceremony marriage. We were given the honor of the first seats. The lectures began with instructions on how to be married in the traditional way; then how to be married in the white man's way, since it was being enforced among the Navajos. The ceremony was recorded for future evidence of marriage for the couple and their families. Also, we stressed the necessity of obtaining a marriage certificate.

Chapter 17

# Warehousewoman and Other Jobs

Late one evening a man appeared at my door.  He handed me a
key and said, "*Shimá*, my mother, here is the key to the warehouse.  The
grains are on the way in so many trucks.  Take care of it from now on as
warehousewoman.  I cannot find anybody competent to take over."

Thus began my job as warehouse keeper at $1.50 an hour.  I was
in charge of distributing grain and hay to livestock owners in districts
10, 11, and 12.  It was a real job for a woman.  I worked day and night
during the drought disasters.  I handled the monies received from hay,
and took care of all the bills of lading.  Feed was hauled in from Gallup
at night, and issued during the day.  There was always someone at my door
at all hours of the day and night.  This went on for about three years.

Our warehouse was an old wreck of a store building.  No floors
at first, and no lights.  I used flashlights.

In winter time I was out in freezing temperatures, counting feed
as it was unloaded.  I had charge of hiring and usually I was successful
in getting responsible and dependable men, but there was always friction
among those competing for the jobs.  Some people put in complaints about
me for being hard to get along with.  That was because I wanted order
during the issuing of the feed.  Always there were those who pushed and
grabbed, fearing the feed might run out before they got any.  One man
tried to get me fired so he could take over the job, but the boss from
Window Rock let the chapter know that I was hired by the tribe, not by
the chapter.  I was deeply grateful for his support.

During the years I was secretary I held two other jobs.  The
first was for the Children's Welfare Federation.  I received clothes, old
and new, which I sold for a few cents apiece, sending the money to the
central office in Window Rock.  In addition, I assisted the county welfare worker in taking applications of persons needing help--old age
pensions, aid to dependent children, and disability aid.  Also, I took
welfare applications to the Navajo Tribal Welfare Office for funds for
lumber and other housing materials, prefabricated houses, and emergency
situations.  Such assistance was available to the very poor, ailing, and
disabled.

The other job was district loan representative to the Tribal Council for districts 10 and 11. When a loan officer came out I went with him to the homes of the people to check on their loan accounts. We also took new applications which were handled in a confidential manner. I enjoyed both of these jobs very much.

I also worked on the emergency work-relief program, or what we call "Ten Days' Labor." It has been of real help to the people and has brought about many improvements for our homes, farms, irrigation projects, and dirt roads. The first projects included construction of counting and branding corrals, dipping vats, and small shelter houses along the roads for public school children, and the fencing of cemetery grounds. More recently, the weaving of rugs has become the main project.

At the beginning women did light work along with the men. Women truck drivers hauled materials for the work; some helped plaster houses; some were foremen of projects. I remember my first public work assignment as a foreman for a weed-eradication project. I took two groups of Chinle women, two groups from the Valley, one group from Canyon del Muerto, and one group from Canyon de Chelly. We hoed, pulled, raked out, and burned weeds. We had fun and worked hard, and we always seemed to meet up with snakes. One time a large spider chased me. I screamed and ran, falling over some bushes. Finally one woman took a rock and smashed the attacker, as the others roared with laughter. I had not run like this for some years and the next day I was sore from the experience.

At lunch time we ate our Navajo food: flat-bread fried, corn-bread cooked in hot ashes, and mutton meat which is delicious when it has cooled. Everything tasted good out in the open air. Besides, we had the fun of telling about events here and there, and joking.

In those days I had no aches and pains, nor did I catch colds. When the project ended in November I had a sun-darkened skin and plenty of vitality.

Chapter 18

# A Voice in Our Government

Thanks to John Hunter, Navajos who are unable to go to the Tribal Council in Window Rock can have a voice in their government through their chapters, and can take an active part in solving individual and community problems.

My husband said the Chinle chapter was organized in the home of a Navajo at the junction of canyons del Muerto and de Chelly in 1926. There were many people who attended this meeting, old influential leaders like Frank and John Mitchell and Old *Chishch'illí* (Curly) who gave talks. A man by the name of *Hosh* (Cactus or Thorn) Brown took charge of the meeting. After the talks an informal election took place. As each man was named for an office there was unanimous approval. Elected chairman was *Hastiin Tah* Tlishman; vice-chairman, Jake Brown; secretary, Phillip Draper. Afterwards each gave a speech. All served their full term of four years.

The chapter met at various designated places in the Valley area: Chinle, Canyon del Muerto, Canyon de Chelly.

"At first the chapter was weak," my husband said. "Meetings were not for Navajo advantage, but for government workers to carry on the work among us."

During the early days some of the chapters did well and some did not. The Bureau of Indian Affairs helped the officers carry out their jobs, which pertained to improvement of their land and stock. By the time I took office in 1948, the Bureau had withdrawn much of its help in order that the Tribal Council could assume more responsibility. It seemed to me that our chapter was rather weak at that time. In general, however, chapters gained strength as the tribe took in money from its various resources such as oil, lumber, and uranium.

This money also made it possible for many boys and girls to complete their educations. There is an urgent need for their leadership in chapter activities.

Nowadays, as I observe the good achievements of our educated young people, I realize how ill-equipped were the schools of my time. Yet, in spite of everything, how fortunate I was to be able to serve my people in my community for 15 years.

# Chapter 19

## My Father's Story of Changing Woman

The story of our mother, *Asdzą́ą́ Nádleehé* (Changing Woman), was told to me by my grandfathers of *Táchii'nii* (Red Soil) Clan. I was young and careless then, and did not listen attentively. Now I wish I had. But I will tell what I do remember about how Changing Woman came to be a great miracle in those early days when *Dine'é* were beginning to live in their land.

There is a place called *Dinéhtah* (Among the People) on a holy hill, and this is where Changing Woman was found as a baby girl by some holy people. As they drew near to her a cloud lifted and her body became radiant with light and bright colors. She was very beautiful.

The holy people argued about who should take the baby and raise her. Among them was Coyote, but he was refused because the other holy people had heard him say he was going to eat her. There were some giants who also wanted to destroy her. First Man became alarmed that harm would come to her if a decision was not made quickly and he asked his wife, First Woman, to take her. First Man and First Woman were very wise and good, so the other holy people were satisfied that they should raise this baby girl.

When Changing Woman reached *kinaaldá* (puberty), First Woman made a big occasion of it by calling all holy people to attend and bless the girl. During this four-day rite, Changing Woman was instructed by First Woman and other holy people about home duties and other special teachings for women. Each day she raced—four times—east, south, west, and north. This was to give her physical endurance. Also, she ground a large quantity of the best white corn which had been brought by the holy people. During the last night of the ceremony, while the corn was being baked, the people sang their Blessing Way songs for her well-being—a long and mature woman's life. Everyone enjoyed this important occasion, and First Man and First Woman made a vow that the *kinaaldá* Ceremony would be binding for all young girls.

Changing Woman was a beautiful virgin, much admired and sought after by those who saw her and wanted her for a wife. One day Sun God visited her while she was out in the forest picking up firewood. She fell in love with him and refused all her other suitors. After much courting, Sun God married her and they had two sons, *Naaghéé Neezghání* (Enemy

Slayer) and *Tóbajíshchíní* (Sired by Water). These boys, like their
mother, had been born for a good purpose--to save *Dine'é* from all their
enemies in the land who made their life miserable on earth.

Some say the boys grew to manhood in four days; others say 12
days. They were reared by Changing Woman with the help of First Man and
First Woman, and became strong men who could escape monsters and giants
and other evil ones who made the people miserable. Giants were the offspring of former peoples who lived bad. *Dine'é* were terrified of these
evil ones who were killers with no sense of right and wrong, and who were
always after children. In every hogan there was a hiding place, usually
near the fireplace or under a grinding stone, where parents could hide
their children to keep the giants from finding and eating them.

Changing Woman had to hide her boys from *Yé'iitsoh*, a big
giant who was fond of her. The day he came the boys were hidden under the
grinding stone. The giant saw tracks and gruffly wanted to know whose
they were.

Changing Woman said, "Those are not real human tracks. See! I
made them like this with my hand and made tracks and put toes on them.
I do this because I am very lonesome and long to have children."

The stupid giant believed her and went away, but the boys were
very worried after this. The older one, Enemy Slayer, thought of a plan
to slay all the giants which he told to his brother Sired by Water. Together they confronted their mother and asked who their father was.

Changing Woman replied, "You must not ask such questions because
your father is not human, not on this earth."
"Well," said Enemy Slayer, "I must know who is my father so tell
me."
"If you must know," said Changing Woman, "the Sun God is your
father."
"Fine," said Enemy Slayer. "I shall go see him for I am thinking of getting help from him to slay all the giants that torment us, even
the monsters. All evils."

Changing Woman thought the plan very foolish. She said, "Forget it all. Furthermore, your father Sun God is mean and far away in
heavens where there are dangerous barriers so no one can see or get near
him."

Enemy Slayer and Sired by Water paid no further attention, and
left to begin their long journey to the Sun God. It is said they met
many obstacles. It was very dangerous and they saw many skeletons of
the people who had traveled that way and met their death. Since they
were the children of Changing Woman, the animals and the holy people knew
them. Also, their mother prayed for their safety day and night. All the
animals they met helped, and the little holy wind always whispered in
their ears what to do as they came to each dangerous obstacle. In this
way they came to the very door of the palace where they were given a
magic feather and an iron bar by Lady Spider and Mr. Frog.

They thought Mr. Frog very odd, but held back their feelings as much as they could in order to be polite. However, Mr. Frog guessed and said to them, "Yes, indeed, I am very odd, my Grandchildren. You see my body is round, my stomach is huge and bulgy, my legs are like arrows shot into my body. My skin is rough and bumpy. My eyes are swollen and puffed out. My throat is saggy and puffy. But I am a useful creature to you if you need me."

Both Mr. Frog and Lady Spider had been helpful with their gifts to the boys of a magic feather and an iron bar. When the boys got ready to try the palace door, the little holy wind whispered to them to use the iron bar. The heavy iron door opened easily, for the iron bar was really a bolt of lightning. There were four such doors to the main room where Sun God lived with his wife. Each was opened with the iron bar.

Sun God's wife was very much upset to see the boys, for they were human beings and very small in her sight. She was stern and harsh to them, and wanted to know what business they had coming from earth to Sun God's home, for no humans were allowed inside or even near the palace.

"We came to see my father," said Enemy Slayer.

Mrs. Sun God was so astonished by this statement that she laughed and said, "You puny ones come to see the Sun God, and furthermore claim him as your father. I'll see to this nonsense of yours. Just wait until he comes home from his journey. You'll find out what he is like. He is mean and jealous. He'll kill you."

Just then they heard a loud clanking of armor and heavy footsteps. Instead of letting the boys stand there, Mrs. Sun God told them to hide under the grinding stone. This they quickly did.

Sun God came in, hung his sun on the east side of the room with his shield, and said, "Who were those figures coming to the palace today? Tell, me, is it someone who loves and visits you while I am gone?"

Mrs. Sun God said, "Yes, you are a fine husband! You have been telling me how true you are to me as you go across the earth. Now, these pitiful human beings come into our home and tell me they are your sons. You shall look upon them and know for yourself who came today." With that she lifted the grinding stone, and out they came to stand before Sun God.

Sun God began, "How dare you human beings enter my home. You are not allowed here. Did one of you claim I am your father? Speak up!"

Enemy Slayer spoke up, for he was always brave. "Yes, you are my father. My mother told me so. One day you visited her on earth and I was born four days after."

Sun God did not admit this. Instead he decided upon some hard and dangerous tests for the boys in the hope of doing away with them. First he sent down huge cutting irons of lightning which came fast and

73

close together, but little holy wind whispered just when to dodge.  Then Sun God had them enter a very puzzling zigzagged hall.  He led them far in where they would feel lost and unable to make the proper turns to get out, but the little holy wind helped them find their way back.

Sun God then decided upon an even harder test, and asked them to make the correct reply to what he was thinking.  Again the little holy wind assisted them.

"You are thinking of the four holy mountains in The People's country," they said, and went on to name all four of them.
"That is correct," said Sun God.  "Now for the last test to prove you are my sons.  Come with me out to the back of the palace."

There they saw a sweat house built out of all kinds of precious stones and fine dirt, with a black rain-cloud hanging over the doorway, a bolt of lightning, and a rainbow.  The stones for the sweat bath were made red hot and put inside and the boys pushed in with them.

After awhile, Sun God asked them if they were warming up.
"Yes," they replied, "we're enjoying it."
A few moments later, he asked, "Are you hot?"
"Yes," they answered, "we are just fine."

Then Sun God got some water and threw it on the hot stones.

Someone said to the boys, "Quick!  Dash in that hole behind you and close your selves in with that rock there."  This they did.  From this enclosure they could hear the hot steam.  Finally the sizzling ended as the stones cooled.  As they peeked out, Sun God asked if they were all right.

"Yes, we are fine!" they yelled.

Sun God removed the door cover and let them out.  Putting both boys under his arm, he said, "You are truly my sons.  Come now, we will go back to the palace room.  There I will entertain you, and then you must go for I cannot stay here all the time.  I have work to do to keep the earth lighted and warm."

The boys were ordered to get fixed up for the feast.  Sun God told his wife to clean and work on Enemy Slayer; Sun God's daughter was to fix up Sired by Water.  They were cleaned up and given a physical treatment until they resembled their half brothers, sons of Sun God and his wife.  Both of their half brothers had thick black mustaches.  To make the boys look manly, too, they were allowed long mustaches which turned up at the ends.  They were dressed handsomely in fine clothing and jewelry, and felt very big and strong while they feasted on all kinds of good nourishing food.

After the feast they were asked what gifts they would like best.  The east portal was opened and they were shown a white cave full of white beads, buckskins, buffalo robes, fine furs, belts, blankets, and so forth. To the west was a turquoise cave with good food from plants, wheat, corn, fruit, and nuts. To the south was a pearl cave of horses, cattle, and useful animals. To the north, there was a jet cave, with sheep and goats.

Sun God said, "You can have anything your heart desires to take back with you, but your mother, Changing Woman, has all these riches, too. You may not see this, but she is rich, too. Down there, if you or any Navajos pray for these things, they can have them."

Enemy Slayer replied, "All those things are fine and good for us, but we do not want them. We came to ask for just one important thing of you."
"What is that?" said Sun God.
Pointing to bows and arrows hanging over the east door, the boys said, "That is what we want and need to slay our enemies, the giants especially."
"Oh, no," said Sun God. "You cannot kill those giants for they are your brothers. They are human just like you."
The boys answered, "That we know they are, but they are very bad."
Sun God continued, "Furthermore, you cannot have those weapons. They are not for human beings to use, for they are sacred and strong with bolts of lightning and will destroy everything, even you."

However, the boys kept begging for bows and arrows until Sun God yielded and showed them how to use them, saying, "You will still need my help in handling these weapons. Now, don't linger any longer. Get on the arrow and I'll shoot it right down to the center of your country. See your mother down there?"
"Yes, we see her," said Enemy Slayer.
"See the strongest, meanest giant over by the lake, ready to drink--the one that walks on his head? You will land near him. He will have to be the first one slain. If you succeed you will be able to get rid of the others very easily."

Down the boys went on the lightning arrow. It is said that Enemy Slayer hesitated to get on the arrow for he didn't trust it, and that Sired by Water had the courage to step forward and get on first.

Sired by Water said to his brother, "Ha, ha. You have hesitated. You have lost your advantage. I shall be the one to slay our enemies."

Father Sun God laughed over this incident as the boys were hurled to earth with all speed. As soon as they hit the ground they began to kill all the enemies who had distressed them for so long. During this time, Changing Woman kept constant vigil. She had a long white beaded stick which she held up to the sun. When there was smoke at the end, she knew they were in danger. When drops of blood appeared, she knew they had killed another enemy.

When the boys thought they had killed all their enemies, they spied some who had overtaken them without being seen. Also, they noticed a strange light far off against a mountain which looked like a fire. Every time they tried to go toward it they lost their way. Finally, they stuck a stick in the ground just ahead of them and leveled a pointer straight toward the fire. In this way they were able to follow a straight course which took them to it. There they found a dugout hogan with a cedar bough for closing. They removed the bough and went inside where, to their surprise, there were sleeping figures.

One figure woke up, rubbed his eyes, and said, "Oh, so Enemy Slayers are here. We hear that you have killed all the giants and other evil monsters. Now here I am." Throwing himself at their feet, he said, "Kill me, too, for I am Miserable Poverty. If you kill me the clothes you have on will never wear out and you will be filthy in them as long as you live. You will not enjoy new clothes nor an increase in food."

The boys thought it best to let him live, so we still have poverty.

The next figure to wake up was Sleepy, who yelled out, "Kill me, too. If you do you will always stay awake and there will be no rest for you." The boys, who had become sleepy, decided to let him live.

Then Old Age awakened, hobbled up--old, wrinkled, and shaking-- and squealed, "Kill me. If you do you will always stay young and there will be no old people to turn to for wise teachings." They let him live so we have old age with us.

Next was Death--pale, cold, stiff-looking--who said to the boys, "Kill me, too, along with other enemies. For if you do you will not die. Children will just be born and multiply until there will be no place for all the living. I am your friend, even if you know it not." So they let him live.

Then the boys came to Mr. Lice. A louse got on them and they began to scratch. The louse said, "Let me stay with you--on you. Don't kill me, please. I will be your pastime when you have nothing to do-- when you are lonesome. Keep me for amusement." So they did not kill him, and now the Navajos have lice.

Next was Cold, who said, "Kill me now. If you do it will always be hot; no snow, no water, no cold breeze when you want it. How terrible this would be." So the boys thought about this and decided to let Mr. Cold live.

When the boys returned home they found their mother sitting inside the hogan. "We're home, Mother," they exclaimed.
"You scared me," said Changing Woman. "Where do you come from, my grandchildren?"
"We're your children," said the boys. "Don't you remember us? We have come back from our father and have even killed all the giants and other evil monsters and known enemies."
"I do not believe you," said Changing Woman, who had not

recognized the boys because they were so improved in every way. "Besides, who could kill them all for they are beyond our strength."

"Oh, yes, we have," said the boys. "Come, Mother, and see the head of the *Ye'iitsoh*, the big giant. The greatest of all giants has his head hanging on the tree out in front of our hogan."

Changing Woman looked upon the head, then said, "My children, my brave sons, you have killed him. Today I am happy, for I shall never fear the old evil ones again. Now my children can live in peace and happiness." Then she grabbed the sword from one of her boys, stuck it into the giant's head, and began to dance about as she sang a song about an increase of riches for her people.

The medicine men know this song, which they sing during the Enemy Blessing ceremony to cure the patient of illness by driving out evil spirits.

[The story of Changing Woman was Irene Stewart's favorite story because it was about the beginning of her people. Many years later, her husband Greyeyes told her how the clans originated, though this is by no means the only version. Because the origin of the clans has been transmitted by word of mouth, there are variations in all the stories. Greyeyes's version follows.]

After the boys killed all the man-eating giants and monsters, First Man and First Woman called a council meeting of all the gods and holy people, even animals. For in those times the animals talked and could be understood by other people as well as gods. To *Ch'óol'į'* (Lookout), the holy place, came the people who had not been killed by giants and monsters. Changing Woman suggested that the first Navajo hogan be built wherein more *Dine'é* could be born. It is said that corn of all kinds, flowers, pollen of plants, and dew drops were used to make this hogan. Changing Woman rubbed sweat and dead skin or scales from her body to make figures of human beings. From her feet came a man and a woman to begin the *Kinyaa'aanii* (Standing House) Clan; from over her heart came the *Tó'áhání* (Near Water) Clan; from her back, the *Hashtłshni* (Mud) Clan; and from the palms of her hands she made the *Tódích'íi'nii* (Bitter Water) Clan.

There were other people living in the land nearby who acquired the names of the places they lived as clan names, or from some habit such as the *Bit'ahnii* (Folded Arms) Clan, or from a people, like *Naakaii Dine'é* (Mexican People).

When the making of more *Dine'é* was finished on *Ch'óolį́í*, the gods and holy people sang our great Blessing Way songs and Changing Woman, whose other name was *Yoołgaii Asdzą́ą* (White Bead Woman), went to live far away at the Ocean in the West. She took the four major clans as far as *Tsin Bel'ahi* (Forest Mountain) near *Dooko'oostłį́į́d* (San Francisco Peaks).

77

On *Tsin Bel'ahi*, Changing Woman gave instructions how to keep the clans breeding to produce strong offspring. She begged the clans to be good and faithful, and to pray always to the West where she dwelt. "I will hear you and help you," she said. Then she gave her farewell speech and prayer, and sang 12 songs of parting from her people. This is said to be the most sacred, the last of the true religion as it was revealed to our people.

# From My Notebooks

## by Mary Shepardson

In rereading my Chinle field notes, which go back now for almost two decades, I realized that there were incidents--scraps of information, quotations from others--that Irene had not put into her story. I have tossed these together in a kind of catchall, without too much order or chronology, to round out the picture of this quite remarkable woman who is my friend.

During the campaign of 1955 for the Navajo tribal elections, I interviewed as many Chinle Navajos as possible to sample their opinions on the candidates. When I asked what they thought about Irene, I got such answers as these: "Irene would be good. She's had a lot of contact with white people and knows how to get along with them and you have to be able to do that at Window Rock." "Irene is not partial to anyone. The menfolks, though, they are partial."

A former Navajo judge said, "The majority of Navajos around here would rather elect someone who will let them do what they want, but Irene would be better than the councilmen we have. She doesn't drink or gamble."

The postmistress said, "Irene is a very reliable person. She has worked a lot for social welfare. She would be good."

A Navajo employee of the Bureau of Indian Affairs said, "Irene Stewart lives near Garcia's. She doesn't have a full-time job because she hasn't been well. She has worked a lot in community services and the people around here know her. She has a good reputation and the most education of any of the three candidates. She has been Chapter Secretary, President and Vice President of the PTA, and on the School Board. She has really helped the older people."

The cook at the Indian Boarding School, where I was eating during my study, told me that she was very sorry she hadn't had time to register to vote. "I want to vote for Irene. I got interested when I heard the ladies discussing the elections. I'm glad we have a lady running for our Council from Chinle."

The trader told me, "Irene is one of the brightest. But she doesn't reach out much. She could do more. I don't think she electioneered at all."

The Superintendent of the Subagency answered my question about Irene by saying, "She **is a** good community worker. One of the best we have around here. She has high morals."

When Irene lost, I questioned more people. One woman said, "I voted for Irene. I expected her to be elected. Most of the women in Chinle voted for her but the men didn't. She gets on the men for not behaving right when the Chapter leaders have those meetings in hogans to help with the quarrels."

Irene told me, "Annie Wauneka bawled me out for not getting elected. She said, 'I wanted you here working with me on the Tribal Council.' Well, I've been reelected Chapter Secretary so that's where I'll be."

Some of the first talks I had with Irene gave me information about her family. Her father was Jake Watchman from Fort Defiance, of *Táchii'nii* (Red Soil) Clan. His father had been the first night watchman at the Fort after the Navajos returned from Fort Sumner, and that's where he got his name, *Kin yi natałi* (Watching Around the House). He was a *Tábąąhá* (Edgewater) clansman.

Irene's father was called Jake *Tso* or Big Jake. He got the name from railroad men because he was strong and could handle the jackhammer and had the strength to handle the iron rails.

Irene said she had seen her grandmother on her father's side only once. She lived by Cottonwood Pass above Crystal. Irene's mother was from Canyon de Chelly, and her English name was Eleanor Bancroft.

At the west side of Fort Defiance town there are ruins in rock shelters [Irene said]. Up on the ledges are old stone graves--piles of rock either against or under the overhanging rock. When I was a girl at boarding school at the old Fort, on some sunny warm days, usually a Sunday afternoon, we were taken for long walks. During these trips we found dried-up human bones among the rocks. Our elders had told us not to go near graves, much less to look at them, because the spirit of the dead person whose grave it was would bring about illness and death, and the spirit of the dead person would rush us off to the place of the dead. Somewhere among those old rock shelters and graves, my mother lies buried.

My oldest half-sister was named Doris (*Asdzáá Tso*, Big Girl). Her father was *Ma'ii Deeshghizhnii* (Coyote Pass Clan). She was the one who told me that my father wanted me so much to be a boy. My father used to say that if the policeman hadn't taken me to school, I would have been just like my grandmother. I would have gambled just like her and been a wild Navajo. "She would have given you to a rich old man for his wife," he said. That was the custom, to give a young girl to a rich old man as soon as she was able to do housework. They expected a present in return. They liked to have a daughter connected with a rich man. My grandmother moved to Tuba City where my uncle George Bancroft lived. He was educated and had lots of sheep and cattle. Doris married Maxwell *Yazzie*, and my half-sister Anne married a man from Navajo Mountain named *Denetso*. My grandmother,

an uncle, a sister, and my brother Joe all died in Tuba City of the
flu in 1918.

My cousin Rose Watchman was in school with me. She was my
father's brother's daughter. I asked her why they started to call
me "Watchman" over there; in Canyon de Chelly I was called just *Głį*
*nezbah*. She explained about it being my last name. There were
three *Głį nezbahs* so they called me *Głį nezbah* Number One. It was
the missionary, Mr. Black, who took me in when he found I had lost
my mother, who changed my name. He said, "Let's get rid of that
*Głį nezbah* and call you Irene." I liked it. I thought it was pretty,
but my father didn't like it. He called me *Głį nezbah* till his
death. My half-sister, Madalene, by my father's second marriage,
was named *Ałnááyibah* (They Passed Each Other While Going to War).

Later I became acquainted with Madalene who lived on the canyon
rim. She was inordinately fond of animals--dogs, cats, even ducks--and
she collected many of the strays about Chinle. She and her husband were
migratory workers who had gone all over California and Idaho following
the crops. Irene, too, had her animals. At one time she had seven horses.
"My boys are crazy about horses," she said. "I suggested that they turn
them in and get goats on the grazing permit. They wouldn't hear of it."

Long before I studied anthropology, I used to visit Chinle with
my late husband, Dr. Dwight Shepardson. One weekend in the early 1940s,
we discovered Thunderbird Lodge. We planned to spend the night in Chinle,
visit Canyon de Chelly the next morning, and return to Gallup, New Mexico,
in the afternoon. The moment we stepped into the beautiful living room
which the traders, Inja and Cozy McSparron, had decorated with their rare
collection of baskets, Navajo rugs, antique silver pieces, photographs,
books, and paintings, we fell under a spell. Year after year we returned
to ride horseback in the canyon, to watch the Indians as they came to
trade, to linger at the dining table after Inja's delicious dinner to
"yarn." Cozy, who had lived on the reservation since he was 19 years old,
was a fine story-teller. One of his favorite tales was about an Indian
who had shot a white man. This Navajo holed up in the canyon with his
brothers and sent word to the trading post that he would never be taken
alive. Cozy, in his soft, deliberate manner, savoring the details, told
how he had persuaded this man to give himself up on the promise that he
would help him with the "law." Little did I realize when I listened,
spellbound, that 20 years later I would be listening with the same intense interest to Greyeyes's own version of how he shot the white man.

Howard Wilson, the sheriff of Gallup in 1958, reminisced about
his days on the reservation with his uncle, Cozy McSparron. He had known
Greyeyes at Chinle. Greyeyes had taught him a lot of Navajo. "He shot
a white man, a rough type. Fortunately the man didn't die although he
was shot through the head. I helped Greyeyes out on his case."

When I first met Greyeyes he was already an old man--tall,
spare, with graying hair. Irene said he still had a good singing voice
and that he helped out often with Blessing Way at the Sings. "Other men
his age have lost their voices," she said proudly. Unfortunately when I
first met Greyeyes I did not own a tape recorder, and when a decade later

I recorded his songs from Blessing Way and the song about *Mosi* (Cat), he apologized, saying that he couldn't sing too much any more.

Greyeyes told me that his mother, who was from the Canyon, was born at Fort Sumner. The family stayed there two years after she was born. When his grandmother was returning, she was pregnant again. She got hurt at Fort Defiance where they were issuing rations because the people were squeezing so hard, and she died. Greyeyes said, "My mother brought up my uncle. He was a famous runner named *K'e zhoozhi*. He ran from the Chinle junction to Oraibi once to get a smoking weed for a ceremony, *Dził na'toh*. He got back for the evening, at twilight, just as it was getting dark. He was Big Medicine Man, a *Tábąąhá*, and he came from Del Muerto Canyon."

As a boy Greyeyes was called *Ashkii Tso*, or Big Boy. Later he was called Greyeyes. Then his sister came back from school at Leupp with the name Grace Stewart. So she named him Greyeyes Ben Stewart. That sister married a Mormon, Paul McRae, a white man. They worked at Fort Defiance for 30 years and now are retired, living on their own place, their own land near Mammoth, Utah.

Greyeyes has some difficulty in adjusting to "progress." When Irene had their house electrified, he refused to pay his share of the utility bill because he did not approve of such dangerous things. One evening, Irene's son caught him playing solitaire in the light which came from the other room through the half-open door. "Why, the old man is stealing my electricity," he complained to his mother, laughingly.

Several Anglos had expressed surprise to me that Irene, who was educated and a Christian, could be the wife of a medicine man who spoke no English and was so much older than she. One day, however, the very person who had been the most puzzled by this marriage said to me, "Irene has been telling me how she and Greyeyes walk over the hills looking for plants, and how he tells her stories about old Navajo beliefs and myths. I've come to the conclusion that they *enjoy* each other."

Greyeyes admires and feels protective toward his wife. During the 1966 elections the bitter campaign between Samuel Billison and Raymond Nakai, who were running for tribal chairman, erupted into a fist fight at Wide Ruins. Greyeyes was so much worried that when his wife had to go to Window Rock on business he insisted on accompanying her, a heavy walking stick in hand in case she was threatened. He pleads with her to have a Navajo Sing whenever she is ill.

Each time I returned to Chinle, Irene would be engaged in a new occupation besides her Chapter job. One year she was in charge of the clothing distribution at the Mission. "I like to work at the Mission," she said. "It makes me nervous to sit home and think about my health." Another year she was taking welfare applications for the Navajo tribe. Or she might be the Registrar in the general elections. Once I found her supervising the distribution of surplus grain, the first large-scale tribal enterprise. Another year she was in charge of the women's weed-control project which was part of the public works program instituted by the Navajo Tribal Council with Council funds. It was designed to stimulate local initiative and consequently strengthen the Chapters, the Navajo version of their own War on Poverty.

One of Irene's activities during the forties and fifties was handling disputes and "legal" matters when the aid of Chapter officers was requested.

In those days we used to make wills for people [Irene said]. The family would get together and listen to the will. Relatives would come from far off.

We took up lots of cases, non-support, for example, before they went to court. We didn't have much success with them. Some cases were desertion. A very few of those quarreling people would make up and start living together again, but some couldn't make it. If parents were having trouble with a girl or a boy they would call on us to talk to them. We handled some adultery cases, too. Called in both parties. I remember one case of a wife who asked us to tell a young girl to stop bothering her husband. We talked to the girl and told her not to interfere with the marriage.

We had land disputes and grazing disputes, but now these go to the Grazing Committee. We had a few witchcraft cases but not too many. They are hard to settle. We never could find out the truth. No proof. The person who is accused denies it. We never found anyone digging near graves. Theft cases were hard, too. The people would deny stealing. We didn't investigate any cases; only had to go on what they told at meetings where the families all got together. All this stopped when we got a full-time judge at Chinle. You know him, *Zhealy Tso.*

I well knew the difficulties the officers of the Chapter had experienced in putting the organization back in running condition after it had been allowed to decline. For one thing, the Chinle Chapter had no meeting room. The little house which had been built for the Chapter in the twenties had been taken back by the Bureau of Indian Affairs (Indian givers?) and was being used as a school room. The Bureau, in anger when the resisters to stock reduction voiced their protests at Chapter meetings, withdrew government support.

In the 1950s, the Chinle Chapter met outside, under the trees. I remember one meeting which was held at the side of Garcia's trading post under a cottonwood. The Chapter officers were present, also some officials from US Public Health, a representative of the Navajo Tribal Council, and a few Chapter members. A Health Educator was explaining the vaccination program when great swirls of dust presaged a violent electric storm which scattered the small audience precipitously. It was a great day, therefore, when Chinle finally dedicated its own Chapter House, the gift of the Navajo Tribal Council.

Irene described it to me: "Our Tribal Chairman, Paul Jones, was there, also the Vice Chairman, Scott Preston; Annie Wauneka; Sam Billison; Howard Gorman; and the BIA superintendent, Fred Maxwell. Father Pius gave the invocation and Reed Wenny, our Chapter President, introduced the speakers. Joe Carroll, our Councilman, spoke also. I was disappointed because the Tribal Band didn't arrive to raise the flag. After that we had a community dinner and everyone was happy.  I guess it has been worth all that hard work."

.  .  .

Irene wrote her story to me in the 1960s.  More than ten years have passed and she is still living in her house near Garcia's old trading post.  But she is living alone.  Her boy, Charley, died after years of nursing and suffering from arthritis.  The disease, Irene thought, was perhaps caused by the many injuries he sustained in rodeos all over the reservation.  Now Greyeyes is also dead, but one son and his family live in Chinle and her grandchildren from Phoenix find "Grandma Chinle's house" a favorite vacation spot.  Irene is no longer an active officer of the Chinle Chapter but she is Chinle's representative to the Navajo Nation's Council on Aging.  Tribal programs for elderly Navajos is a recent project, among a number of other social services for which the Tribal Government is taking some responsibility.  Irene, a senior citizen herself, is playing her part as always in the planning and execution of programs to benefit her people.  She says she is a little tired, but is determined to be active as long as her physical strength holds out.

Irene Stewart, 1965.
Photograph:  John D. Wallace

Greyeyes Stewart, 1965.
Photograph: John D. Wallace

Greyeyes Stewart on his beloved (if troublesome) horse, 1965.
Photograph:  John D. Wallace

Girls' Puberty Ceremony, 1956.  The mother moulds the girl.
Photograph:  Franciscan Fathers

Girls' Puberty Ceremony, 1956. The girl blesses a child.
Photograph: Franciscan Fathers

Girls' Puberty Ceremony, 1956. The ritual cake is prepared.
Photograph: Franciscan Fathers

Scott Preston, Vice-chairman of the Navajo Tribal Council,
and Annie Wauneka, Delegate.  Nazlini Chapter House Dedi-
cation, June 30, 1962.
Photograph:  John D. Wallace

Canyon de Chelly. Irene was born in this canyon.
Photograph: John D. Wallace

Spider Rock, Canyon de Chelly.   Spider Woman lives on
top of the tallest pinnacle.
Photograph:  John D. Wallace